THE FORGOTTEN LINK

The research underlying this book was organized by Per-Itaca S.r.l. (Rome) and made possible by financial support from

- Agenzia del Lavoro della Provincia Autonoma di Trento (Labor Agency of the Province of Trento)

- ASAP and INTERSIND (the Italian public sector employers organizations)

- Commission of the European Communities

- ENEA (the Italian Public Agency for Energy and Technology Research)

THE FORGOTTEN LINK

Labor's Stake in
International Economic Cooperation

Richard Edwards
and
Paolo Garonna

Rowman & Littlefield Publishers, Inc.

ROWMAN & LITTLEFIELD PUBLISHERS, INC.

Published in the United States of America
by Rowman & Littlefield Publishers, Inc.
8705 Bollman Place, Savage, Maryland 20763

British Cataloging in Publication Information Available

Library of Congress Cataloging-in-Publication Data

Edwards, Richard, 1944-
The forgotten link : labor's stake in international economic
cooperation / Richard Edwards and Paolo Garonna.
p. cm.
Includes bibliographical references (p.   )and index.
1. Alien labor—International cooperation.
2. Employment in foreign countries—International
cooperation.   3. Labor mobility—International
cooperation.   4. International economic integration.
I. Garonna, P., 1948- . II. Title.
HD6300.E39   1991
331.12'791—dc20   91–11677 CIP

ISBN 0–8476–7676–5 (cloth)
ISBN 0–8476–7677–3 (paper)

Printed in the United States of America

 ™ The paper used in this publication meets the minimum requirements of
American National Standard for Information Sciences—Permanence of
Paper for Printed Library Materials, ANSI Z39.48–1984.

this book is dedicated to

Sam
Elena
George
Adriano
Irene
and
Rebecca

Contents

Acknowledgments

THIS BOOK GREW OUT of a project conceived in Rome on the eve of the greatest political and economic changes since World War II. As the walls between East and West were falling, we believed that it was a good time to examine other obstacles that impede the free movement of peoples. Our work is dedicated to the hope that our children's generation will live in a peaceful world of few barriers and enjoy the great riches of diverse cultures.

Many colleagues and friends have contributed generously to our work; we of course remain responsible for its content. Tim Koechlin, David Marsden, and Paul Ryan wrote important background papers and also provided very helpful criticisms. Carlo Borzaga, Raffaele Brancati, and Makis Cavouriaris also contributed important studies. We gratefully acknowledge very helpful comments and suggestions from M. Alessi, P. De Luca, M. Brutti, C. Sampietro, E. Vitiello, J. W. Morley, P. Varesi, M. Betta, and R. Drago. Kevin Crocker, Antonella Ianni, M. D.

Zampino, and Denny Kalyalya assisted with the research, administration, and other tasks of the project, and we greatly appreciate their generous, intelligent, and highly competent help.

1

The Forgotten Link

THE 1980s WITNESSED the emergence of an increasingly integrated world economy; the 1990s will almost certainly see this process continue and even intensify. Corporations construct their marketing strategies based on transnational, if not global market opportunities. Traded goods and services encounter fewer barriers, either formal or informal, to movement across international borders, and the volume and the importance of trade continue to increase. Stock exchanges, banks, and monetary institutions of all types are increasingly linked in the emerging global financial markets.

Integration has not yet produced a single global marketplace; rather, we would argue, transnational trading areas—the European Single Market, North America, the Pacific Rim trading partners—are increasingly becoming the effective and meaningful economic units. The major trading areas are becoming more integrated internally, and these blocs of developed countries are being tied together more closely in an increasingly dense set of reciprocal economic relationships. For the developed world in particular, economic relations are no longer most usefully conceived of in national units.[1]

The realization of the Single Market in Europe in 1992, the U.S.–Canada Free Trade Agreement, and other similar efforts aim at reducing or eliminating the economic significance of national borders. Coordination of macroeconomic policies has become a primary subject for concern and initiative in the international policy agenda. In all dominant respects, the economic realities of our era push economic agents, whether corporations, governments, international policy-makers, or others, toward adapting to and adopting a transnational perspective. Both unplanned responses to these realities and more conscious policy formulations go toward facilitating the growth of transnational economic relations.

Yet in all this activity there has been a forgotten link: What connects the world of labor to the emerging international opportunities and risks? What is labor's stake in international economic cooperation? Of all the social partners, labor is the one whose betterment has been most weakly and ambiguously tied to the world's developing economic integration. Certainly it is recognized that workers indirectly benefit from the higher rates of growth, greater income, and expanded employment opportunities that globalization may bring about. Workers in fact are also consumers, income recipients, and job searchers, and as such have an interest in economic integration. But do workers also have an interest as workers? Most commonly, the question of workers' interest in increasing integration has by and large been neglected. This is particularly the case with the G-5, G-7, and G-10 activities.[2]

When they are considered, policies to address labor's interests have usually been very narrowly conceived. For example, policy-makers have generally acknowledged that workers may suffer losses from integration—losses that may come in the form of workers being rendered redundant or dislocated by new trade patterns, workers having their skills made obsolete by the introduction of new technologies, or workers being made powerless by the loss or enfeebling of their trade unions—and the discussion has focused on the means to compensate workers for these expected losses.[3]

The G-7 economic summits, to take another case, have failed to look beyond labor-market flexibilities, job creation, and retraining. Even in the comprehensive and forward-looking policy approach of human resource development, labor is looked at as an input to the production process, an object for investment, a source of precious capital, rather than a subject of integration policy, an actor in the world context of increasing interdependence. Rarely in international councils have policies been contemplated or implemented to identify labor's objectives in integration and to facilitate workers' gains from integration.

In planning for the European Single Market, the workers' interests were given more consideration, but even here the official policy-making bodies have only taken up these issues very late, after the trade unions and other workers' representatives have insisted upon official consideration of what impact the Single Market will have on workers. In 1988, the president of the Commission of the European Community, Jacques Delors, made an address to the Trades Union Congress appealing to the members to turn to Brussels for new social advantages, and to stress the importance of 1992. The Commission has also been fairly active in promoting the Social Charter (Europe Sociale). Two main concerns motivate this interest. One is to give greater weight to the Single Market, and the second is to encourage the social partners to begin to see the European Community institutions as another focus for rule-making which is independent of national governments and the Council of Ministers.[4]

So there is today much debate about the "social dimension" of the Single Market.[5] We welcome and encourage such consideration, and surely the issues being raised are of vital importance to the future well-being of the European Community's workers. We agree that there must be satisfactory resolutions to the issues of "social dumping," of how nationally organized trade unions will be able to function within a multinational unified market, of the appropriate standards for workplace health and safety, and of the other questions raised.

But as we suggest below, this debate has reached something of an impasse because the alternatives being considered are too limited in their fundamental presumptions. Rarely if ever have policy-makers specifically addressed the issue of what positive new opportunities and potential new benefits workers may gain from the opening of transnational markets.

This book grows out of the conviction that new and large gains for the world of labor are possible in the processes of integration, and that these gains may be won for labor if our conceptualization of labor's interest is broad enough and our policy-making bold enough. Our work also grows out of a corresponding conviction that the processes of transnational integration, and the benefits derived therefrom by the other social partners and by society at large, can be secured more adequately and with greater stability if labor's legitimate stake in integration is understood, recognized, and respected.

We claim that:

1. Workers potentially have much to gain from international integration, including new types of benefits that have usually not been recognized. The processes of integration open new opportunities and offer new horizons that could greatly enrich the life situations of workers. These new opportunities, however, will not emerge automatically; nor is their appearance inevitable. Moreover, these possible new gains exist alongside the risks and potential losses that workers may also suffer as a consequence of integration.

2. Policy-makers have failed to devise and implement policies that would make the realization of these new prospects likely. Policy-makers and others have been too limited in how they conceptualize the world of labor and they have given too little attention to the claims of labor's interest to institute the appropriate policies.

All too often labor unions have shared this cramped and limited view of labor's interest. They have felt the threats coming from increased international competition, particularly for what it implies for the allocation or relocation of investment. For instance, in some cases multinational corporations have operated as though they could face down attempts by the unions and shop stewards to unite across different European countries by simply threatening to close a vulnerable plant. But the unions on the whole have failed to see and exploit the new opportunities and the potential gains that internationalization could bring about.

3. Recognizing and addressing labor's stake in the integration process will most likely provide some immediate benefits to some of the other social partners, particularly employers. For example, as we argue below, arranging for

the transnational recognition of skills would certainly be in labor's interest, but it would also open to employers in need of qualified workers a broader arena in which to find them.

More importantly, facilitating labor's gains from integration is in the long-run interests of all of the social partners because it serves the larger interest of social stability. Economic integration is likely to work over the longer term only if it appears legitimate in the eyes of workers and the population in general, acquiring therefore a political dimension. For example, European labor needs to benefit from the prosperity that it is hoped will follow from the Single Market; by contrast, exclusion from these benefits could well generate significant opposition. In short, there is reason to believe that the issues raised here have importance and benefits beyond that of simply ensuring labor its due.

This volume is therefore devoted to broadening the conceptualization of labor's interest and to suggesting some of those policies that would be needed to achieve for labor the benefits of international integration. Beyond our specific suggestions, however, we appeal to international policy-makers, trade unions, national economic decision-makers, and others to rethink how their policies may assist the world of labor to achieve its rightful and full participation in the emerging economy of transnational integration.

Labor's Stake in an Integrated Economic World

What interests do workers have in the ongoing trend toward increasing economic integration? Why should workers notice or care about the integration process?

Of course it seems obvious that workers, like all other participants in the economy, will be affected by those forces that influence, for good or ill, the general health of the economy. Thus, for instance, most workers in the industrialized world benefited from the institutional and other arrangements that made possible the long postwar boom; employment, real wages, and other elements of labor's well-being all improved dramatically between, say, 1950 and 1975. On the other hand, many workers have suffered from the troubled economic circumstances of the last decade and a half. Higher rates of unemployment, slower growth in real wages, industrial dislocation, and greater economic uncertainty have adversely affected workers as much or more than other economic actors. Workers no less than bankers or industrialists, then, have a stake in the economy's general health.

Moreover, it is widely recognized that workers' interests are affected in many direct and indirect ways by integration. As consumers, they benefit when a wider variety of goods and services are more dependably and conveniently available at lower cost. As national citizens and taxpayers, they benefit when other contributors to the social system, including employers, are more prosperous and therefore can shoulder a more substantial portion of the common financial burden. As citizens of the world, they benefit when economic growth is more pervasive and geographically widespread, both because we all benefit when our fellow human beings prosper and because, alternatively, growing inequalities threaten world peace. To the extent that increasing economic integration supports better economic performance in these areas, then, workers have reason to support policies that enhance economic interdependence.

Are there, however, more specific and proximal consequences for labor in the integration process? Workers qua
workers appear to have other and seemingly more ambiguous interests in economic integration. It is usually acknowledged that, on the positive side, arrangements that
raise the productivity of labor, for example by permitting
the importation of capital or the transfer of new technologies, will tend to raise the wages of labor and could
improve the quality of working life. So, too, the extension
of the output markets of the employers of labor may result
in a fuller employment, or employments on more remunerative terms, than otherwise.[6]

On the negative side, however, exposure of workers to
wider labor-market competition, including competition
from workers in national markets where historical wage
standards are low, may reduce workers' bargaining power
and result in wage declines.[7] Losses in wages and erosion
of working conditions are especially likely if the increasing
integration results in weakening of trade unions or the
rendering of their organizational reach insufficient for
effective collective bargaining. Similarly, workers may
suffer if increasing integration, by eroding national
sovereignty, replaces it with some form of international
sovereignty—either the international marketplace or international agencies—that is less favorable to workers than
the deposed national ones.[8] In all these ways and other
more subtle and indirect ones, labor evidently has an
important stake in international integration, but whether
labor's interest will be positively or negatively affected by
increased integration remains unclear.

These aspects of workers' interests define the terrain for
the current debate. The balance among these various factors, even whether a particular element impacts positively

or negatively upon workers, remains controversial. Much of this debate has turned on yet another set of influences, the most important of which are (1) macroeconomic policy, and particularly the extent to which macroeconomic authorities permit the full employment and utilization of existing labor resources; (2) the economic gains from international trade, and specifically the degree to which wider trade opportunities foster higher labor productivity; and (3) trade union organization, and importantly the ability or inability of unions to organize and represent workers within a wider and more nationally diverse market.

The discussion in this book ventures outside the confines of this conventional debate. We do not claim that the conventional literature or its policy focus is unimportant, only that it is too limited in its view of the workers' interests. We agree that the traditionally defined aspects of the workers' interests are crucial ones, and we acknowledge that the accepted array of influences upon those interests will remain critical in determining whether workers gain or lose from the growing integration. The fact that our discussion does not focus upon these aspects and influences should not be read as an implicit denial of their significance, because it is not intended as such.

We argue instead, however, that in the processes of integration there are other possibilities, other positive opportunities for labor that should be recognized and could be realized. We believe that a greater effort should be made to identify these opportunities, and that once identified, international policy-makers, trade unions, and national governments should work harder to build into the processes of integration those policies necessary to permit labor to realize its new opportunities.

In the following chapters, our primary focus is on two of these prospects:

1. The promotion of the transnational mobility of workers, to give workers much greater real opportunities to work in and therefore experience and benefit from a wider world market;

2. The encouragement of diverse employments, to sustain workers in their efforts to maintain, promote, and cross-fertilize identities based on regional, occupational, cultural, linguistic, and other loyalties.

We also consider some of the issues raised by a third concern:

3. Migration, especially (a) the management of South–North migration, that is, the movement of workers from the less developed countries into the labor markets of the developed world, and (b) the regulation of East–West migration, that is, the movement of workers from Eastern Europe newly freed as a result of the great wave of reform now transforming the Eastern European countries.

We will explore these themes in greater detail. But they represent only some among the many new possibilities that open to our view when we pose for serious consideration these questions: How can workers gain from increased economic integration? What truly is labor's stake in international economic cooperation?

In what follows we speak of "labor," "workers," and "the world of labor" more or less interchangeably, and we mean by these terms to convey a very broad categorization, including virtually all for whom salaries or wages gained from the sale of their labor-power is their primary means of livelihood. As will be apparent, we distinguish the world of labor from those official representatives (labor unions, labor parties) who speak in behalf of labor. We also use broadly the terms "qualified" or "skilled" workers, to signify those extensive middle and higher layers of workers, including all who have technical skills, who make up the category of educated labor, who constitute the professional and scientific cadres, who have labor-market attributes in high demand because of successful work histories or informal learning, and for whom their labor-market experience reflects this more elevated status.

Notes

1. See for example Richard Belous and Rebecca Hartley (eds.), *The Growth of Regional Trading Blocs in the Global Economy* (NPA Publications: Washington, D.C., 1990). Peter Kenan (*The International Economy*, 2nd ed., Prentice-Hall: Englewood Cliffs, N.J., 1989; Table 1–1) provides the following simple but telling data on the increasing openness of the industrial economies:

Trends in Economic Openness: Averages of Exports and Imports of Goods and Services as Percentages of Gross National Product in the Seven Economic Summit Countries

Country	1965	1975	1985
Canada	19.5	24.2	28.0
France	12.1	18.1	23.7
Germany	19.0	24.9	33.1
Italy	13.4	21.7	26.8
Japan	10.3	13.7	14.5
United Kingdom	18.8	26.3	28.3
United States	4.7	8.0	8.5

For more general reviews, see *Trade and Development Report, 1987* (United Nations: New York, 1987); *World Development Report 1988* (World Bank: Washington, D.C., 1988); and *World Economic Outlook* (International Monetary Fund: Washington D.C., 1986). For a cautionary historical review, see David Gordon, "The Global Economy: New Edifice or Crumbling Foundations?" *New Left Review*, no. 168 (March–

April 1988), pp. 24–64. For the international impact on one labor market, see John Abowd and Richard Freeman, "The Internationalization of the U.S. Labor Market," NBER Working Paper No. 3321 (National Bureau of Economic Research: Cambridge, Mass., April 1990).

2. For example, in the nine final communiqués of the G-7 economic summit meetings from 1982 to 1990, the problems, interests, or opportunities of labor are rarely mentioned. The 1983, 1984, and 1985 statements briefly note the need to enhance productivity, expand job training, and eliminate market rigidities. On other labor topics and in other years, the G-7 leaders were entirely silent.

3. This was the thrust, for example, of the U.S. Trade Adjustment Assistance, first introduced in the Trade Expansion Act of 1962 and significantly expanded in 1974.

4. Throughout the text we will use the slightly imprecise but familiar term "European Community" (or EC) to refer to the new institutions of integration being developed in Europe. There are in fact three "communities," the European Economic Community (EEC), the European Coal and Steel Community (ECSC), and the European Atomic Energy Community (Euratom); of these three, the EEC has by far the most significant economic impact. The executive agency established to administer the communities is the Commission of the European Communities, with headquarters in Brussels. The EC's decision-making body is the Council of Ministers, consisting of a representative from each member government, with the representatives changing according to the subject under consideration. The European Council consists of the heads of state or of government of the member countries and is the highest political decision-making body. The European Parliament, which sits in Strasbourg, has limited legislative and oversight powers. Various other agencies and bodies exist as well.

5. "Social Dimension of the Internal Market" (Marin Report), Commission of the European Communities, EEC (88) 1148 final, Brussels, Sept. 14, 1988 (mimeo); "The Social Dimension of the Internal Market," Commission of the EC, in *Social Europe*, Special Number, Office of Official Publications of the EEC, Luxembourg, 1988. On the wider economic implications of 1992, see *The European Challenge 1992, The Benefits of a Single Market*, Report of the Research Group on the "Costs of Non-Europe" (Cecchini Report), Commission of the EC, 1988 (French edition by Flammarion: Paris; Italian edition by Sperling and Kupfer: Milan); "Communications from the EEC Concerning the Action Programme Relating to the Implementation of the Community Charter of Basic Social Rights for Workers" (Commission of the EC:

Brussels, November 1989). See also (e.g.) "Efficienza Stabilità ed Equità, Una Strategia per l'evoluzione del sistema economico della Comunità Europea" (Padoa Schioppa Report), Commissione della CEE (Il Mulino: Bologna, 1988); "Creating the European Social Dimension in the Internal Market," Confédération Européenne des Syndicats, Dec. 2, 1988 (mimeo); "Maximising the Benefits, Minimising the Costs: TUC Report on Europe 1992" (Trades Union Council: London, August 1988); and Wolfgang Hager, "1992: What about the Workers?" *The International Economy*, vol. III, no. 2 (March-April 1989), pp. 84–88. Gary Clyde Hufbauer, *Europe 1992: An American Perspective* (Brookings: Washington, D.C., 1990). Paul Teague and John Grahl, "European Community Labour Market Policy: Present Scope and Future Direction," *Revue d'Integration européenne*, vol. XIII, no. 1 (Automne 1989), pp. 55–73.

6. Robert Z. Lawrence and Robert Litan, *Saving Free Trade: A Pragmatic Approach* (Brookings: Washington, D.C., 1986), and U.S. President, *Economic Report of the President, 1989* (U.S. Government Printing Office: Washington, D.C., January 1989), pp. 165–67. John Abowd and Richard Freeman, "The Internationalization of the U.S. Labor Market," NBER Working Paper No. 3321 (National Bureau of Economic Research: Cambridge, Mass., April 1990).

7. Barry Bluestone and Bennett Harrison, *The Deindustrialization of America* (Basic Books: New York, 1984); Lawrence Mishel, "The Late Great Debate on Deindustrialization," *Challenge*, vol. 32, no. 1 (January-February 1989), pp. 35–43; Ray Marshall, *Unheard Voices: Labor and Economic Policy in a Competitive World* (Basic Books: New York, 1987).

8. Ken Gill, a British trade unionist and past president of the TUC, put it this way:

> As we see it, 1992 will produce increased dislocation in the unionized sections of European industry as it forces unions into greater international cooperation. This will further concentrate economic power in fewer and fewer hands, as it weakens the ability of a national governments [sic] to intervene in the interests of their own economies and peoples.

"Europe 1992: The British Response," *Economic Notes* (Labor Research Association), vol. 58, no. 5–6 (May-June 1990), p. 9. See also Barbara Barnouin, *The European Labour Movement and European Integration* (Pinter: London, 1986). Denis MacShane, "Trade Unions in Europe in the 1990's—Challenges, Opportunities and Dangers" (mimeo; International Metalworkers Federation: Geneva, March 1989).

2

Removing the Formal Barriers to Labor's Transnational Mobility

WHY SHOULD INTERNATIONAL agreements and cooperation promote the movement across national boundaries of all the elements in the economic process except labor?

Decades-long negotiations have aimed at making easier the international flow of traded goods and services, capital, technology, innovation, management, financial instruments of every type—in short, of every economic input or output except labor. Mobility restrictions are less severe for the most unskilled labor (who in any case often migrates illegally or clandestinely) and for the very top of the highly skilled category (for example, managers). But for the majority of workers in the broad middle categories of skilled or educated labor, for workers whose labor is generally in demand, the barriers are highly limiting. Removing these barriers has not been a high priority; in the discussions of the Uraguay Round of the General Agreement on Tariffs and Trade (GATT), for example, or in the OECD or the Group of Seven or Group of Ten, freeing such labor to move internationally has rarely been raised.[1]

Should international policy promote the transnational mobility of workers? Yes, we argue in this and the next chapter: workers have much to gain from the opportunity for transnational mobility, and cooperative policies to promote economic integration should not omit labor. Moreover, the costs—to all the social partners — of artificial restrictions on labor mobility are likely to increase as the other elements in the economic system become more integrated. As a recent U.S. government study concluded, "as the United States and Canada enter an era of free trade in the 1990s, the tensions between increased trade and limited legal immigration may become acute."[2] Increasing economic integration should encompass all the principal elements of the economic system.

At least among the workforces of the developed world, workers ought to be able to move easily from employment in one country to employment in another. And as in the case of promoting trade, capital flows, and other forms of integration, policies to promote labor mobility must go beyond the mere abolition of formal barriers to cut away the informal barriers to labor movement.

We are concerned here with promoting the opportunity for workers to take up employment in other countries. But workers' rights to migrate for jobs have often been conflated with two other issues: migrants' rights to become citizens in the receiving country, and migration motivated by other reasons. Our intent is to explore the right to seek employment abroad, but first we must briefly consider the other two issues.

Labor Mobility and Citizenship

There is no logical necessity for workers who take up foreign employment to gain access to citizenship in their new residence. What we argue below is that workers should have the right to geographic mobility in search of employment. Whether any particular host country also wishes to offer access to citizenship is, we believe, best left to the decision of that country. Our point is that whatever naturalization policies individual countries may choose to adopt, those decisions need not imply restrictions on labor's right to geographical mobility nor barriers to the effective integration of workers in the host country's productive community. We distinguish between, on the one side, a worker's opportunity to seek employment in and to participate under conditions of nondiscrimination in the life of another country, and on the other side a migrant's access to citizenship, because the issues raised by each are quite distinct. This point is not, however, uncontroversial. One recent thoughtful study flatly declared: "Over the long run, in a democratic society, residence and citizenship should roughly coincide."[3] The question we pose is simpler and politically much easier: why not free labor to find its best employment? Thus we might imagine a new regime in which workers in the developed countries would be free to move among these countries in search of their most preferred work, all the while remaining citizens of their "home" country, but having access to the same basic rights as the "host" country workers.[4]

The question of whether an immigrant must be granted the right to become a citizen of his or her new country of residence has become highly charged. A recent collaborative study argues strongly for the right. William Rogers Brubaker and his colleagues examined immigration, "denizenship" (permanent residence status but without citizenship), citizenship, and naturalization in six North American and European countries.[5] They document the rising numbers of residents in these countries who have secure status as "denizens" but who lack full citizenship rights.

Brubaker and his associates offer a model of "two concentric circles" to describe modern-day membership in the political and social community. The inner circle includes only citizens; the outer circle also includes "denizens," that is, permanent resident aliens and, in Europe, residents who are citizens of the other European Community nations. Those in the outer circle can participate in most of the economic, social, and cultural activities of the community, and they have a virtually nonrevocable right to remain in the country, but they are denied participation in the political process. Members of the "inner circle" reserve to themselves the right to vote ("to take direct part in the formation of national policy"), the right to employment that involves the exercise of public authority, and the "duty of military service." On grounds of democratic theory, they argue that this situation is unsatisfactory. In Brubaker's words:

> As a way station on the road to full citizenship, denizenship is desirable. But in the long run, denizenship is no substitute for citizenship. [Host countries] must transform their denizens into citizens, enjoying political as well as economic and social rights. Nothing less is required by their self-understanding as democracies.[6]

We would not necessarily dispute the desirability of opening citizenship to migrants, but this change confronts overwhelming political barriers, and we believe it should not be the obstacle to block other and useful reforms.

Migrants' access to citizenship naturally invokes issues of cultural, linguistic, and ethnic identity, of political cohesion, and of the meaning and content of nationality. These matters touch deep historical and social-psychological currents, making consideration of them tricky and unpredictable in outcome. Some countries, like the United States and Canada, with long traditions of welcoming large numbers of immigrants to become citizens, may wish to continue this policy; others, like most of the European states, may wish to restrict access to citizenship. These differing historical traditions, and the current naturalization policies that continue them, need not preclude progress on labor's rights to mobility.

Moreover, the urgency of placing high priority on naturalization and citizenship rights is limited by several considerations, many of which are pointed out by Brubaker and his colleagues. In an increasingly open and integrated world, citizenship itself has become less crucial in defining one's membership in the civic world. Brubaker notes that "citizenship status is not what matters most in the economic and social sphere" and "citizenship status is in fact relatively insignificant as a basis of access to social services."[7] Peter Schuck examines recent developments in constitutional law and finds a "devaluation" of American citizenship, that is, a reduction "almost to the vanishing point [of] the marginal value of citizenship as compared to resident alien status"; he argues that this devaluation "is not—on balance—a cause for great concern" and is in any event probably irreversible.[8]

Finally, the premise underlying this whole line of argument, that migration will be permanent, applies to only part of the migrating population. This premise reflects the current high barriers to movement, barriers that are worth overcoming only for relatively permanent moves or for those clandestine migrants willing to evade the legal restrictions. Yet just as workers now exercise substantial and growing geographical mobility within national labor markets, so too the relaxation of transnational mobility controls is likely to result in an increase of what might be called intermittent or multiple migrations rather than permanent migration. Such multiple movements, with continuing ties to the "home" community and country, seem especially probable for successful job-holders of the broad lower and middle ranges of occupations.

Thus we believe that access to citizenship is not necessarily a sine qua non for enhanced mobility rights. Access is likely even to prove irrelevant for many migrants, including, we believe, an increasing number of those workers who would benefit from enhanced mobility rights. "Citizenship" raises very emotional and rather ideological issues. It evokes the notions of national identity, of cultural and historic ties, of ethnic pride. These notions have provided the foundations upon which modern nation states have been built and have developed in the last three centuries. But they have also fomented separation and antagonism, and have often justified the erection of all kinds of impediments to labor mobility and to equal opportunities. We think that the issues of citizenship can and should be kept separate from the more pragmatic ones of ensuring to workers the opportunity to move, the freedom to search for employment where they want, and the dignity of seeing their basic rights recognized everywhere. For these reasons we believe it is more fruitful to separate the discussion of migration from that of citizenship.

Migration for Other Reasons

As we have seen during the past century or two and continuing in the present, many people move from one country to another for reasons other than to seek additional work opportunities. They may be impelled by such motives as avoiding religious or political persecution or reuniting with family members. Our discussion below does not deal with "noneconomic" migration, and policies to regulate this migration are and probably should be rooted in principles different from those considered here.

Labor's Stake in Transnational Mobility

Do workers care whether they have the right to seek employment in other countries? And even if they do not care now (because, say, present barriers offer them so little chance to experience it), would they come to value it if given the chance? After all, if workers do not or would not, should not international policy-makers pass on to more pressing issues?

We know of course that there is a huge pent-up demand for access to the developed countries: the massive illegal migration that persists despite extensive border controls is evidence of that demand. But this is primarily a demand for movement from low-income to high-income countries; what about the implicit or potential demand for mobility among the industrialized countries? The demand here is harder to gauge, because existing barriers prevent movement and workers from these countries are less likely to risk illegal migration.

National and international policies governing worker

migration do vary, however, and in a few instances labor has been included in the efforts to make international borders more porous. The European Community is undoubtedly the most important case, offering to workers the right to seek employment anywhere within its boundaries.[9] Yet this relatively recent *de jure* right has not resulted in very substantial movement by EC workers to take up employment elsewhere. One recent study placed the degree of "interpenetration" of EC labor markets (that is, the number of EC workers employed outside their home country divided by the total employed labor force) in 1980 at just 2 percent.[10] Individual country data, for the mid-1980s, show similar patterns. In France, for example, workers from other EC countries made up just 3 percent of the labor force; in West Germany and the Netherlands, about 1 percent. More revealing is the fact that in France and the Netherlands, foreign workers from non-EC countries outnumber those from the EC; and in West Germany, non-EC workers outnumber non-German EC workers by better than 3:1. Only in Belgium (with 6 percent of its labor force from the EC) and Luxembourg (29 percent) has the attraction of EC workers added significant proportions to the local workforces, and special conditions obtain in these (small) countries that explain their anomalous situations. Evidently, being granted the formal right to take up employment elsewhere in the EC has not resulted in substantial transnational relocation.[11]

The conclusion that removing formal barriers provides only a modest de facto boost to transnational mobility in the EC is also revealed by other data. For example, consider the data on migrating workers from Portugal and Spain, countries that joined the EC in 1986. For both countries, the number of workers sent to other EC nations *declined* after their admission to the EC; yet during the same period, the number of Portuguese and Spanish migrants who went elsewhere in Europe (for example, Switzerland) *increased*. Greek workers employed elsewhere in the EC also declined after Greece's 1981 entry, although the quality of the available data is poorer. Moreover, during the period when the EC employment of Greek, Portuguese, and Spanish workers was declining, the number of Turkish workers employed in the EC increased and those from Yugoslavia remained approximately constant. Although special transition-period rules have delayed full EC migration rights for Spanish, Portuguese, and Greek workers, they do not seem to explain this pattern.[12]

Undoubtedly these various shifts and trends are influenced by many and complex determinants, and we shall not attempt to sort them out here. But the easiest ways to dismiss the relevance of these data can apparently themselves be dismissed: The post-EC-admission decline in Greek, Portuguese, and Spanish workers employed elsewhere in the EC was evidently not due to a general decline in EC labor demand, else why would Turkish and Yugoslavian employment in the EC grow? The decline also seems not to have been due simply to rising labor demand in these countries' domestic labor markets, since labor exports (at least for Spain and Portugal, for which we have data) to elsewhere in Europe increased. When Greece, Portugal, and Spain entered the EC, the abolition of the formal barriers to labor migration did not much change the actual movement of workers, and perhaps the safest conclusion would be that the formal barriers are not the principal impediments to increased migration. Indeed, Willem Molle and Aad van Mourik concluded:

> Contrary to what migration theory would predict, the elimination
> of legal barriers to migration has not produced a great increase of
> migratory flows. On the contrary, migration among Member
> States has decreased since the Rome Treaty became effective.[13]

In the EC, eliminating *de jure* barriers has resulted in relatively minor de facto intra-EC migration; elsewhere, however, strictly enforced legal barriers have resulted in highly controlled labor flows. In Japan, for example, entry of foreign workers has long been highly limited, and foreign workers represent a miniscule proportion of the labor force. In Austria, employment of foreign workers has been controlled by a system of work permits and a collectively bargained quota. In the 1960s, as Austria's labor needs increased, the proportion of foreign workers also increased; in the 1970s, as higher unemployment loomed, the quota was successively cut and the proportion of foreign workers greatly declined. And in North America, the substantial migration in both directions between Canada and the United States in the 1950s and 1960s was greatly reduced, first by restrictive U.S. laws imposed in 1965 and then by Canadian restrictions in 1976.[14]

Thus we find that while eliminating formal barriers to labor migration does not necessarily greatly increase transnational movement, the existence of barriers can limit it. The elimination of formal barriers seems to be a necessary but not sufficient condition for migration.[15] Even in the EC case, however, where the formal barriers to labor's movement have been eliminated, the informal barriers remain formidable.

The argument for extending the opportunities for mobility not only to goods and capital but also to labor could come from conventional economic principles. Extrapolating from the standard resource allocation arguments used to encourage the mobility of other economic factors within global markets (or labor within regional or national labor markets), this response argues that the size of the market constrains the potentials for increasing specialization and productivity. The world economy is experiencing a period of growing interdependence among the national economies; world trade and capital mobility are growing at an unprecedented rate; trade barriers are being eliminated and the international diffusion of technological innovations is rapidly increasing. Hence, one might conclude, labor markets in these circumstances also ought to adjust by eliminating artificial market barriers; skilled labor mobility would then be a necessary corollary to a more general movement toward a freeing up of all markets.

This argument points in the right direction and is not unpersuasive, but it is inconclusive and somewhat naive. Possible gains in allocative efficiency seem puny when set alongside the political, sociological, national security, and cultural differences creating divisions across the globe. Besides, there are limits and costs to increased specialization, such as those highlighted by the work of industrial sociologists on alienation, or more crudely on absenteeism, turnover, and poor motivation, and those analyzed by industrial economists on small firms and subcontracting.[16]

A conventional view arguing against encouraging the mobility of workers, one that is often advanced most strongly by national labor movements, is that, except for workers who are unemployed or with few skills and a bleak future, the workers themselves do not want to move and so opening the frontiers would only increase competition for jobs. Workers have strong family and cultural ties to their place of residence; those workers who are successfully placed in stable, reasonably remunerative jobs would seem to have too much to lose from migration, in terms of status and prestige, in their labor-market position, in command over economic resources, and in their living standards. In fact, all workers—according to this conventional view—lose from moving, but some of them, obviously the weaker, less-well-placed ones, are compelled by economic necessity to leave.

We claim that this point of view is misguided. It is roughly equivalent to saying that "the poor have no taste for luxury goods" and therefore do not buy them. For workers other than those compelled to move, it expresses a panglossian attitude toward the world as it is. It neglects the fact that workers' ties to their places of residence are often "involuntary" and depend on a variety of constraining factors (for example, housing relocation costs; or more generally, all the adjustment costs related to the change of residence, including the difficulties of integration into different educational systems, unfamiliar social patterns, and so on). It is of course true that the most substantial movements of labor across national frontiers involve people who have little to lose, that is, young and unskilled workers. But to interpret this state of the world as an equilibrium situation corresponding to people's judgment of their welfare is an arbitrary assumption. It assumes perfect information and rational choices but ignores the artificial constraints imposed by current laws and policies.

We would advance an opposite point of view, one that has at least as much empirical foundation as the conventional one and a view that we find more persuasive. Workers, if the constraints were removed, would choose to be much more mobile than they are at present and would participate much more fully in the benefits of a transnationally integrated economy. Workers, and especially successful labor-market participants (workers with good employment histories and prospects; skilled, educated, or qualified workers; workers whose labor is in substantial demand) are now prevented from exploiting the full potentials of their labor by the existing formal and informal barriers to mobility. Such barriers prevent workers from demanding greater international labor-market integration.

If the opposite view were true—if workers would not value transnational mobility even if given the chance—then why is the existing apparatus of mobility controls necessary? Indeed, the existence and continued support for such controls must be rooted in an implied recognition of our view.

One could in fact hypothesize that the "implicit demand" for migration greatly exceeds the migration now realized. Some preliminary considerations in support of such an hypothesis might include the following:

1. At the very top of the skilled labor force, the executives, managers, professionals, and highly qualified technicians seem to gain a lot from moving abroad. Their command of high incomes and significant resources permits them to overcome existing obstacles and shows what is required *rebus sic stantibus* to compensate for these barriers.

2. If the "variety hypothesis" works when applied to consumption, why should it not work in production? And further, why should it not be equally persuasive when applied to the greater range of choice in living situations and cultures opened by geographical mobility? It is widely agreed that the internationalization of product markets has

positively affected the living standards of the working classes by greatly diversifying and thereby enriching the market basket of goods available to workers; the opportunity to consume imported goods and services (including holidays abroad) alongside home-produced goods represents an enrichment of their living standards. The same advantage would seem to exist with respect to the geographical diversity of jobs and of living situations.

3. The integration of product markets has shown that the benefits of international trade (as revealed by the actions of the traders themselves) derive as much from, if not more than, intraindustry trade as from interindustry trade. It is not only Carrara marble and Vermont maple syrup that are being traded: Italian machines are sent to America and American machines are exported to Italy. International flows of skilled labor are similar to intraindustry trade, and may be expected to develop similarly and to confer similar benefits.

4. Clandestine or illegal migration is substantial, suggesting at least that the demand for migration is considerably in excess of that legally permitted. Indeed, a recent official study of U.S.–Canada migration observed that "it must be recognized that given the proximity of the two countries, limited work permits, long-term 'vacations' of retired persons, and undocumented immigration may well serve as partial substitutes for formal immigration."[17]

In conclusion, it is perfectly reasonable to assume (or in any case it is not less plausible than assuming the contrary) that if skilled and other well-established workers were actually offered concrete opportunities for transnational mobility at substantially reduced (explicit or implicit) cost, they would seize these opportunities and "effectively demand" greater labor-market integration at the international level. Arbitrary barriers raise artificial costs that inhibit this movement, and such barriers should be eliminated. For other costs, the nonartificial or "real" costs that also inhibit movement, intervention may also be appropriate. Where these costs are high for the individual worker but subject to substantial economies of scale, for example, collective (public policy) measures can appropriately reduce the cost to individuals.

The "forgotten link" has created a vicious circle of isolation and localism: To begin, policy-makers' neglect of labor's stake in economic integration has produced substantial formal and informal barriers to the mobility of skilled labor. Next, labor under these conditions does not demand the right to move and perceives mobility as an economically disastrous or distant possibility. Then the circle is closed when labor's failure to demand mobility legitimizes the policy-makers' original neglect.

We cannot expect the vicious circle to break up by itself. We either take it as an equilibrium state, as does the conventional view, or we challenge it by proposing new policies that actively promote the real possibility of the transnational mobility of workers.

Removing the Formal Barriers

A policy to promote the international mobility of labor presupposes those changes in law and immigration regulations required to make such migration possible. We will briefly outline what of substance is necessary, but we will not consider in detail the technical, legalistic, and administrative aspects of such changes.

It would be unreasonable now to propose the full and

immediate opening of all national borders to labor. The
great differences in level of development, incomes, and
labor histories and expectations, not to mention national
political and security considerations, make such a change
unrealistic and even undesirable. But such considerations
do not preclude an arrangement among the most developed countries—those nations, for example, comprising
the Group of Seven, or the Group of Ten, or the countries
included within the European Community together with
the U.S.–Canada Agreement, or perhaps most appropriately, the member states of the OECD. Although clear
differences exist among them, these nations share roughly
comparable levels of development, of living standards, of
protection, and of expectations for labor. They all have
well-developed systems of social welfare, and they have
established and compatible democratic political systems.
These similarities suggest that opening their borders to
cross-national labor mobility would primarily result in its
intended consequences and would minimize other, adverse
and unintended, consequences.[18]

Consider then a situation where by agreement among,
say, the OECD countries, labor was free to move throughout the OECD territory in search of its optimal employment. Workers could retain citizenship in their "home"
countries. Such a system would operate on the basis either
of requiring no visas and work permits within this territory or (perhaps more realistically) of requiring visas and
work permits but making them as easily obtainable for
workers as tourist visas are at present. The conditions
necessary for such a system to operate effectively are that
member states could not arbitrarily limit the number of
visas and work permits granted (for example, because of
local labor-market conditions), and that any criteria for

the refusal to grant such visas and work permits (for example, for public health or national security) limit administrative discretion to the minimum prescribed reasons. Thus, workers would be able to search out and take best advantage of the employment opportunities opened to them in the wider market.

There exist at present multinational and bilateral agreements and individual national policies that approximate the arrangement we propose above. Most importantly of course, workers within the European Community can migrate for work within its borders without formal restriction. Movements elsewhere, for example transatlantic migrations in both directions based on temporary work permits, are not insignificant. Thus the removal of formal barriers to labor's mobility, although in conception and potential magnitude vastly different from current policy, has already in many respects been presaged by existing policies and practices.

Removing the formal barriers to labor mobility is a necessary condition for such mobility, and without such a change, other policies discussed below would be nugatory; but it is not sufficient. As in the case of the European Community, where the removal of formal barriers has led to surprisingly little cross-national mobility, so too we would expect that the removal of the formal barriers to mobility within a wider area such as the OECD countries would be unlikely by itself to have great real effect. Appropriate policy should also seek to reduce the informal barriers to migration. The experience of removal of mobility barriers in Europe might teach us another lesson: that barriers may contribute to stimulation of an artificial and dysfunctional form of mobility that ceases when those barriers are eliminated, that is, the mobility of those very unskilled and marginal workers who operate in the black or informal labor market and whose attractiveness to employers relies only on their being "underground," with no rights or claims. It is remarkable but little noted that liberalization in Europe seems to have been effective in protecting weak labor from exploitation, whereas mobility barriers, often justified by consideration of workers' protection and equity, have sometimes been counterproductive.

Notes

1. A possible exception is the role of the OECD in the mid-1950s when a "Code of Liberalization of Manpower Movements in Europe" was agreed to and implemented.

2. U.S. Bureau of the Census, *Migration between the United States and Canada*, Current Population Reports, Series P-23 (U.S. Government Printing Office, Washington, D.C., 1990), p. 5.

3. William Rogers Brubaker, "Membership without Citizenship: The Economic and Social Rights of Noncitizens" in William Rogers Brubaker (ed.), *Immigration and the Politics of Citizenship in Europe and North America* (University Press of America: New York, 1989), pp. 145–62.

4. Movement between the poorer countries and the developed ones raises other issues that we deal with in Chapter 5.

5. Brubaker (ed.), *Immigration* (for a convenient summary of naturalization requirements, see Table 2); and "Immigration and the Politics of Citizenship," *TransAtlantic Perspectives*, no. 20 (Autumn 1989), pp. 7–10.

6. Brubaker, "Membership without Citizenship," p. 162.

7. Brubaker, "Membership without Citizenship," pp. 146, 155.

8. Peter Schuck, "Membership in the Liberal Polity: The Devaluation of American Citizenship" in W. R. Brubaker (ed.), *Immigration*, pp. 51–66.

9. For brief reviews of EC regulations, see Willem Molle and Aad van Mourik, "International Movements of Labour under Conditions of Economic Integration: The Case of Western Europe," *Journal of Common*

Market Studies, vol. XXVI, no. 3 (March 1988), pp. 318–21; and Paul Teague and John Grahl, "European Community Labour Market Policy: Present Scope and Future Direction," *Revue d'Intégration européenne*, vol. XIII, no. 1 (Automne 1989), pp. 55–73.

10. Molle and van Mourik, "International Movements," pp. 336–37.

11. Figures for France, West Germany, Belgium, and the Netherlands for 1987, for Luxembourg for 1984. *SOPEMI 1988* (OECD: Paris, 1988); Labour Force Statistics 1967–1987 (OECD: Paris, 1989).

12. Unfortunately, the removal of informal barriers has attracted little official interest (with the exception of the CEDEFOP initiatives on mutual recognition of diplomas).

13. Molle and van Mourik, "International Movements," p. 336. Thomas Straubhaar comes to a strikingly similar conclusion: "The legal liberalization of labour movement did not significantly stimulate intra-EC-6 migration flows, compared to migration flows from outside the Common Labour Market into the EC-6. Mobility among the EC-6 members has hardly increased since the formation of the Common Labour Market." Thomas Straubhaar, "International Labour Migration within a Common Market: Some Aspects of EC Experience," *Journal of Common Market Studies*, vol. XXVII, no. 1 (September 1988), p. 54.

14. See Helga Duda and Franz Tödtling, "Austrian Trade Unions in the Economic Crisis" in R. Edwards, P. Garonna, and F. Tödtling, (eds.), *Unions in Crisis and Beyond: Perspectives from Six Countries* (Auburn House: Dover, Mass., 1986). U.S. Bureau of the Census, *Migration between the United States and Canada*, p. 1.

15. The text refers to *legal* migration; obviously illegal migration represents a different case. As M. Cavouriaris (*PerItaca Report*, 1990) notes, "migrations clandestins" are very large now and likely to become more significant in the future. In the case of Japan, a large proportion of the foreign workforce is reported to be illegal entrants.

16. See F. Butera, "Mutamento dell'organizzazione del lavoro ed egemonia," *Economia e Lavoro*, vol. VIII, no. 1 (January–February 1974); S. Brusco, "Labour Market Structure, Company Policies and Technological Progress: the Case of Italy," in O. Diettrich and J. Morley, (eds.), *Relations between Technology Capital and Labour* (Commission of the European Communities: Brussels, 1981); S. Brusco and C. Sabel, "Artisan Production and Economic Growth," in F. Wilkinson (ed.), *The Dynamics of Labour Market Segmentation* (Academic Press: London, 1981).

17. U.S. Bureau of the Census, *Migration between the U.S. and Canada*, p. 5.

18. The enormous and continuing changes in Eastern Europe raise the possibility that at some future date these countries could be included as well.

3

Reducing the Informal Barriers to Labor's Transnational Mobility

TO PROMOTE LABOR's de facto right to seek employment abroad, it is not enough to eliminate the formal barriers. The remaining obstacles, informal or pragmatic hindrances that prevent mobility, must also be reduced.

The practical need for removing the informal barriers inhibiting transnational economic activity has been clearly understood in other spheres. In the case of capital or traded goods, when formal barriers have been removed but informal obstacles remained to intervene and frustrate the hopes for increased integration, international policy-makers have energetically rushed in to dismantle the informal barriers as well. Hence we see efforts to harmonize tax systems, stimulate common insurance requirements, guarantee reciprocal recognition of patents and copyrights, and make consistent all manner of legal, accounting, and marketing rules. We applaud this recognition of the fact that successful integration requires not only the removal of laws proscribing transnational commerce but also positive actions to support removal of informal barriers. But why should not the same lesson be applied to labor?

What has been little attended to is removing the substantial informal barriers to labor mobility. Often these barriers arise out of profound social and institutional differences that cannot be bridged by mere convention, agreement, or supranational regulation. For instance, in spite of the fact that medical doctors' qualifications are already recognized in the EC, there appears to have been relatively little intercountry mobility. But in other cases it appears that these barriers are a more artificial contrivance, resulting from policies and, in principle, removable by policy.

In this chapter we consider two important informal barriers: the worker's difficulty in having his or her skill recognized when abroad; and the worker's uncertainty about and ineligibility for social security protections when abroad. In each case we investigate why the barrier exists and how it could be reduced.

Making Skills and Qualifications Transferable

The transfer of skills and skilled labor across national boundaries is a formidable task, and the difficulties in gaining acceptance for one's skills when abroad constitutes one of the main informal impediments to the integration of work and workers in the international economy. A skilled worker residing abroad is like a naked king, stripped of the accoutrements that make him (or her) recognizable.

The creation and transmission of skills are highly complicated tasks in general, even within national or local labor markets. The reasons for this difficulty are in the nature of skill itself. A skill, in economic terms, is not simply a specific technical aptitude; rather:

1. A skill is an ability that may be technical or non-technical depending crucially on the context to which it is applied. Only by having control over this context (that is, in the work process and the labor market) is it possible to ensure that a specific ability has a predictable positive impact on economic performance and labor productivity.

2. A skill can be developed in many and different ways, depending on individual inclinations and motivations, on various forms of training, on work experience, and on different possible combinations of the three.

3. Finally, a skill depends crucially on the way the corresponding ability is socially evaluated, recognized, and accepted. In fact technical abilities can be evaluated in different ways in different social contexts. These differences can be explained by technological and organizational factors, but also by the development of social norms that affect the structure and hierarchical stratification of society. It is well known that the correspondence between the structure of skills and job content and the hierarchical organization of society is problematic and variable. The great variance of wage differentials by sector and by profession across different labor markets and national economies is a good case in point.

The socially determined nature of skills thus implies several requirements for any effective system providing for the transfer of skills. Such a system would need to control the work processes and the labor markets in such a way that an ability can have a comparable impact in different contexts. It would need to control the mechanisms of reproduction of that ability so that it can be ensured that in given circumstances it is a specific ability (or kind of ability) that is produced and reproduced. Finally, it would need to make sure that the social recognition of that ability is comparable in different contexts, in terms of position of power and prestige in the labor market and in the social structure, in terms of command over resources, etc.

Given these requirements, it is not surprising to acknowledge that the institutional systems currently in place to ensure the transfer of skill within a labor market are complicated and sophisticated. David Marsden and Paul Ryan, following a well-established pattern in the literature, refer to two prototypes of skill transferability institutions: The first type, termed an *occupational labor market*, is based on institutions of apprenticeship and skill standardization that have developed for workers in an occupation and that exist independent of particular employers. The second, called an *internal labor market*, occurs where the acquisition and transmission of skills is internal and specific to an enterprise, mobility between markets is limited to the initial and unskilled positions, and later job moves generally involve downgrading. Considering their impacts on labor-market functioning and performance, both models have been at times praised and condemned, though for inverse reasons, since they give rise to incompatible kinds of flexibility.[1]

The occupational labor market has allowed a relatively high turnover of skilled labor within well-defined, and normally organized, labor segments, but it has also created demarcations and rigidities. More recently, under the pressures and the adaptations required by the introduction of new technologies and by industrial restructuring, there has been a tendency to dilute the skill content and deemphasize the skill dimension of the occupational labor-market structure (for instance, the reduction in the number of recognized qualifications in the German labor market).

The development of internal labor markets has accompanied the expansion and diffusion of large enterprises in mass-production markets, especially where other systems of recruitment and mobility were weak (for example, apprenticeship systems, occupational labor markets). Firms have chosen to invest substantially in the acquisition of skills and in the internal transmission of skills between and among members of their own labor force. Through the mechanism of the internal labor market, employers have provided incentives to promote continuous training and skill upgrading within the enterprises; this market has been structured so as to shelter skilled employment from cyclical swings, avoiding the wastage of skilled labor in economic downturns. But on the other side, internal labor markets have prevented the interfirm and intersectoral mobility of skilled labor, have created problems at the ports of entry and exit into the internal markets (joblessness for young workers, long-term unemployment for older displaced workers, and job instability for both), have imposed costs (for example, downgrading) on workers who move, and have created other rigidities.

In considering the two paradigmatic models of skill transmission, important sectors of the West German and British labor markets probably best exemplify the occupational market model and parts of the Japanese, Italian, and French labor markets exemplify the internal market model. Importantly, these differing organizations of production occur within sectors using similar technologies, and so evidently technology is not the sole determinant of labor-market organization. The literature provides evidence of both relatively good and relatively bad labor-market performance for each of the two paradigmatic models.

In a policy-oriented and prescriptive framework, the importance of the taxonomy should not be taken to lie in the provision of rigid stereotypes that have to be mechanically copied and applied to all kinds of different contexts. On the contrary, the analysis of occupational and internal labor markets shows how comprehensive and wide-ranging those models have to be in order to determine an efficient skill mobility mechanism and a favorable impact on the labor market. The occupational market model, to operate at its best in regulating skill mobility, as it does in the German case, requires a high degree of institutional integration, a developed system of employees' and employers' organizations in the labor market (in some cases an effective neocorporatist structure), possibly also "encompassing" unions, and in any case a strong system of centrally regulated labor-market management and training policies. But other cases also exist. In Britain, for instance, the apprenticeship system has worked well without a neocorporatist link between unions and employers. The internal market model, to be most effective, as it has been in the Japanese case, has required paternalistic management practices, a socially accepted double-tier labor market, and various other elaborated features. Here again variations exist. In Japan, the internal market model has been matched to the predominant system of enterprise unions. In the United States, this model has sometimes depended upon strong union participation at the firm level. In France, the unions tend to negotiate the rules governing internal labor markets at the national level (for example, the agreements on hierarchical job and pay classification systems).

A skill transfer system, to be sensitively organized with respect to its implications on the social structure, on the culture and organization of the labor force, and on the institutions of the labor market, needs to be developed gradually "from within" and "from below." The difficulty of incorporating in one system features that belong to other systems has become quite apparent when traditional occupational labor markets have had to adapt in order to cope with the greater flexibility of skill requirements induced by industrial restructuring in the 1970s. The same thing appeared when internal labor markets had to open up to pressures for greater labor turnover in the labor market in response to pressures arising from mismatches and structural imbalances.

So far we have considered the question of mobility of skilled labor in general. Obviously the comprehensive nature of the systems of skill transfer becomes even more significant when mobility crosses the boundaries of national labor markets. The heterogeneity of social structures, of cultures, and of the systems of industrial organization then becomes a severely constraining factor. These difficulties can be seen in some of the attempts at internationalizing the best functioning models of skill transmission. For example, Japanese multinational enterprises have often experienced substantial problems when attempting to organize internal labor markets outside of Japan. And CEDEFOP, the Berlin-based European Institute for Training Policies, is finding great difficulties in defining certain basic skills in its attempt to apply at the European level the methods of the German apprenticeship system.

The discussions around "Social Europe" and 1992 seem to be going decisively in the direction of confronting the obstacles to migration. Unfortunately, an insufficient understanding of and attention to the forgotten link mars this effort, and the problem of skill transferability constitutes one of the central obstacles. European policies, both at the national and at the international level, are still far from adequate for the purpose of bringing to the surface and giving voice to the implicit demands of skilled labor with respect to this problem.

Looking at the policies that are being put forward in relation to the European integration process, and that are described in Marsden and Ryan (1990), we can identify two philosophically conflicting policy approaches to skill transferability. On one side, there are attempts to define and impose, from a central level, standards, institutions, and regulations that would have to be enforced and respected at the decentralized level. This is the strategy behind the effort to harmonize skill definitions used in specifying training requirements and job descriptions. On the other side, there is the principle of mutual recognition, whereby each country or region is left free to define the skills as it wants, leaving to the market mechanism the sorting out of the best practice.

Both strategies, notably in the case of Europe, have proved unsatisfactory. "Harmonization" has usually implied imposing from above an abstract scheme, derived from the arbitrary simplification and codification of a working system of skill transfer, to different contexts and labor-market cultures, creating rigidities or risking ineffectiveness. "Mutual recognition" has produced a kind of law of the jungle among skill definition systems, resulting in the survival of the strongest, but this strategy has not necessarily produced the system most efficient and effective in meeting labor's needs. "Mutual recognition" of skills is likely to mean in fact that employers and their workers would be left alone in the determination of the exact meaning of a skill and that they would have to rely on expensive trial and error mechanisms. The likely result would be little real opportunity for skilled labor mobility.

The fact is that there generally is not one best practice, to be followed in all contexts. Efforts to enforce such uniformity would result in higher, not lower, costs where the prescribed one best practice did not fit. And on the other side, if as is likely there are significant external or nonprivate costs inherent in establishing an effective system of skill transferability, such a system would not necessarily emerge by itself. Private employers would not be willing to incur the costs, given that a significant proportion of them could not be recouped. Neither of the present strategies would thus produce the optimal outcome.

Ultimately it is not necessary to standardize for the one best practice (whether imposed by the market or by regulation); rather it is sufficient to produce effective translation and communications systems. What is required is an active international skill transfer policy, based on developing transparency and communication mechanisms among different transfer systems, and promoting and supporting selectively the mobility of skilled labor across national borders. The idea of "transparency" developed by Marsden and Ryan goes in this direction: it is intended in fact to raise the information level so that employers could better assess the true technical quality of skills. What specific form the policies to achieve these ends should take is a matter for further research and experimentation. But a few guidelines should be kept in mind:

1. Training must be a fundamental part of this strategy. But it should be considered as a component of a wider and more comprehensive policy of active skill transfer. This

has important repercussions both on the actual content of training and on the relationship between training and other aspects of social, educational, and industrial policy. For instance, language and cultural education should be a necessary complement to technical coaching. And training should be related to career patterns and relocations.

2. Workers' and employers' organizations should be involved through bargaining or social dialogue in building up and implementing mechanisms of skill transfer.

3. Financial incentives and services for individual skilled workers geared toward supporting their mobility should be established at the international level. For instance, expatriation allowances could be in part provided by public money, or low-cost language and civilization education could be offered, especially for workers going to underprivileged areas or regions.

4. Human resource policies should be coordinated with trade and industrial policies. For instance, the promotion of transnational small and medium-sized enterprises could represent a viable mechanism for encouraging international skilled labor mobility within internal labor markets. Another example is the support for the establishment of international associations or professional organizations of skilled labor. This would be probably more effective in creating the conditions for the structuring of occupational labor markets at the international level than any technocratic efforts at harmonizing the definitions of the corresponding skill.

Ensuring Social Security

Workers who consider migrating across national borders often face a second informal barrier of intimidating proportions: the uncertainties of their rights and eligibilities under nationally operated social security or social support systems. Migrating workers should be provided adequate information and guaranteed quick and convenient access to social security benefits.

"Social security" here means any and all of the programs that have been established to assist workers or their families during periods, or for specific circumstances, when families cannot adequately provide for themselves. Included are benefits for medical care, sick leave, maternity care, disability loss, old-age pensions, survivors' income, loss of work due to employment injury, unemployment compensation, and family allowances.

The extent of social security protection varies considerably among countries, even among the developed countries. Some social security programs provide all of the above-mentioned benefits, whereas others provide very limited benefits. The varying levels of benefits, and the diverse eligibilities for them, cause confusion about the availability of benefits in the receiving country.

Among the developed countries, a thick network of mostly bilateral agreements governs the social security treatment of a worker from one country employed in another country. In general, those programs for which contributory payments are made (by workers and/or employers) or for which employment ensures eligibility have been made reciprocal. An American working in Italy, for instance, and having payments made in his or her behalf to the Italian pension system, upon returning to the United States can apply for and be granted credit through the American social security system for those payments. These social security agreements usually contain special provisions, called totalization clauses, for workers who are not employed long enough in any one country to fulfill minimum work credit requirements; totalization agreements permit a worker to combine work credits earned abroad to meet the requirements for insured status. Each country then awards a pro rata benefit depending upon the amount of work performed under its system.[2]

There also exist some multilateral arrangements. Certainly the most important is that initiated by the Council of Europe.[3] The European Convention on Social Security established a system mandating uniform treatment and access to benefits for nationals of the contracting states when resident in another of the contracting states. Thus, for example, a German worker employed consecutively in France, Italy, and the Netherlands will earn employment credits toward an old-age pension that will be based on his or her employments anywhere within the ambit of the contracting parties. The convention also establishes principles of uniform treatment (nondiscrimination against resident foreign workers from the contracting states) with respect to most social security programs. Such treatment has become quite routinized.

The legal arrangements both within the European convention framework and more generally are less clear than they would seem at first glance, however. There is no international system to provide truly uniform treatment, since so many of the arrangements are covered by bilateral agreements, each with its own peculiarities. This is the case even within the European convention framework, where social security supports that are means-tested or not related to contributions are likely to be covered by bilateral agreements rather than multilateral ones. Thus, invalidity, old age, and survivors' or occupational disease benefits derive from generalized plans, whereas family benefits, unemployment compensation, medical and health coverage, and maternity benefits are likely to be subject to bilateral arrangements. And outside the European convention framework, bilateralism is the rule. For example, to be eligible for a totalized benefit, a worker must satisfy a country's minimum work credit requirement, a criterion that varies among countries. Moreover, such agreements almost invariably contain unique restrictions. In the U.S. case, for instance, the agreements permit a worker to count credits from only one other country.

Bilateralism simply compounds the already highly complex character of national regulations governing social security benefits. Social security eligibilities are especially complicated and cumbersome. They involve extensive special regulations, voluminous files and record-keeping, differing enrollment and probation periods, and arcane exemptions and qualifications. They are administered in every industrialized country by a bureaucracy that is extensive and intricate.

The typical worker normally encounters this dense thicket of social security regulations and institutions in his or her own country little by little over the course of a work life—enrolled in some programs at birth, others when entering school, others at the first job, at marriage, at first payment of direct taxes, a parent's retirement, and so forth. The result is that such workers, even those who are poorly educated or uncomfortable when interacting with large bureaucratic entities, develop over time an extensive fund of knowledge about social security agencies. Moreover, they can draw upon the assistance of friends, relatives, fellow workers, trade unions, church or social contacts, and others to help them gain their rightful social security benefits.

When a worker migrates across a national border, his or her connection to the social security system changes dramatically and adversely. The worker suddenly needs a great deal of new information, and he or she is simultaneously deprived of the knowledge reaped from personal history or available through friends and relatives. The result is an intimidating information gap.

The worker needs to know, at one point in time, how to enroll in all the relevant programs. He or she confronts a new system, with different rules, expectations, requirements, bureaucratic culture, even a different language, and typically he or she has little knowledge about this system. The worker's ability to draw personal assistance from surrounding resources—the experience of co-workers or the support of knowledgeable relatives, for example—is vastly diminished.

All too frequently, the worker who chooses to migrate also chooses simply to live and work outside the receiving country's social security system, except to the extent that contributory taxes are automatically deducted from his or her pay. Given the vast information requirements needed to negotiate this passage successfully, inadequate knowledge of and anxiety about social security benefits must inhibit many would-be migrants.[4]

Is the provision of social security necessarily so complex and so nationally idiosyncratic that there can be little relief from the burden placed on migrating workers? In fact, the International Labor Organization (ILO) has on several occasions attempted to address this issue.[5] In diverse conventions, including most directly Convention 118 (Equality of Treatment of Nationals and Non-Nationals in Social Security), the ILO has sought to promote exactly the kind of international system that might facilitate worker movement by encouraging member nations to provide protection and equal treatment in social security for non-national migrants. Convention 118 obligates each ratifying member state to grant to non-nationals "equality of treatment under its legislation with its own nationals, both as regards coverage and as regards the right to benefits. . . . "[6] This convention thus establishes the fundamental first principle—equality of treatment of non-nationals with nationals—required to construct a transnational system of social security. This first principle has been supplemented by other conventions, or parts of conventions, to flesh out a fuller system of protection:

1. Equality of treatment for refugees and stateless persons regardless of the territory in which they are resident (Convention 118);

2. Criteria for determining which national legislation is applicable, to avoid conflicts of laws, multiple required contributory payments, overlapping benefits or gaps in benefits (Convention 157, Maintenance of Social Security Rights);

3. Rules for the maintenance of rights already acquired by virtue of residence in a member state (Convention 157);

4. Rules for the maintenance of rights during the period when the worker is in the course of acquiring or becoming qualified for rights (Convention 157).

But while the ILO has led the way in articulating the need for and devising principles to guarantee social security to non-national migrants, it has been much less successful in persuading member states to follow its leadership and achieve actual protections. Convention 118 was launched in 1962; by 1990 thirty-six nations had ratified it, but many of those are countries whose social security systems provide minimal benefits (for example, Cape

Verde, Mauritania, Bangladesh, Bolivia). Not all the industrialized nations have ratified the convention, and among those that have, many have chosen to exclude certain portions ("branches") of the convention. In general, they have ratified those parts that guarantee equal treatment in the provision of contemporaneous benefits for currently employed workers and excluded those parts that extend to more long-range benefits. The Federal Republic of Germany, for instance, ratified those branches covering medical care, sickness benefits, maternity, occupational injury, and unemployment; it excluded those branches requiring equal treatment with respect to disability benefits, old-age pensions, survivors' benefits, and family allowances. Some countries, like Italy and the Netherlands, ratified the entire convention, while many others, including the United States and the United Kingdom, have not ratified any portion. Convention 157 was initiated only in 1982 and has so far gained even less acceptance.[7]

Bilateral agreements, and multilateral agreements where applicable, clearly do provide migrating workers with certain rights. Some rights tend to be relatively common, at least among the industrialized countries: equality of treatment with respect to sickness benefits, access to medical care (where socially provided), maternity rights, and employment injuries. On the other hand, extension of rights to disability compensation, old-age pensions, unemployment benefits (especially depending upon residency), and family benefits tends to be much more spotty.[8] Moreover, serious gaps exist for workers for whom migration is a temporary interruption in their careers rather than a permanent change of location. For these workers, it is more problematical to obtain credit toward old-age, unemployment, and family benefits, to determine which national legislation will be controlling, and to avoid compulsory contributions to multiple systems.

Despite the ambiguities and difficulties inherent in the legal arrangements, potential migrants are probably much more deterred by the informal barriers to achieving social security protections in the receiving country. These barriers include lack of information and the uncertainity it creates, lack of documentation, difficulty in dealing with social security agencies, and language and cultural differences.

Perhaps the greatest barrier is simply the lack of information available to the typical potential migrant. Before migration, the potential migrant usually must make do with information available in his or her own country. But frequently this information is scarce, costly to obtain, incomplete, and indefinite. The various bilateral agreements and even the European convention have resulted in far more attention being paid to the needs of reciprocal bureaucratic functioning (for example, proper accounting for contributory payments made) than to providing those aids that would facilitate workers' actual ability to migrate. Information required by a worker considering migration may be available only through an embassy or consulate, and rarely is it packaged comprehensively so that a potential migrant can determine the full range of benefits for which he or she and accompanying family members will be eligible. These difficulties may be overcome by the largest employers; for them, it may be economical to collect such information for their workers or workers they are seeking to recruit. But for small and medium-sized businesses and for individual workers, such obstacles are more forbidding.

A further obstacle is documentation. Nationally distinct systems of documentation—birth certificates, marriage licenses, earnings and income histories, medical records, occupational licenses, schooling records and qualifications certificates, withholdings claims, tax filings, and so on—result in bureaucratic demands for documentation that is correspondingly diverse. The potential migrant must be able to produce appropriate documentation sufficient to establish eligibility, in circumstances where cross-national interpretation and acceptance of documents of foreign issuance are likely to be begrudging.

Difficulty in dealing with social security agencies compounds the barriers. Migrating workers are confronted with large, impersonal, and complex bureaucracies, too often staffed with overworked and insensitive officials charged with carrying out the complex social regulations. For such officials, dealing with foreign nationals seeking benefits often constitutes an unwanted additional burden. Because of language problems or lack of familiarity with specifically national features of bureaucratic culture, foreign workers typically do not know the relevant regulations, may have difficulty filling out even the simplest parts of forms accurately, need special help and attention, and require, because they are foreign, the official to apply arcane and little-used laws. Little wonder that the migrating worker is often not met with a welcoming reception.

Finally, of course, language and cultural differences pose their own obstacles. While such barriers are intrinsic in transnational mobility, their practical effect may be heightened by the typically arcane and legalistic vocabulary universally adopted by social service bureaucracies. The lack of special resources devoted to assisting the migrant worker through the maze of social security regulations and administrative apparatus typically leaves the migrant at the mercy of functionaries for whom such migrants are an unwelcome addition to normal workloads.

Given the diversity of national systems, each with its distinct menu of benefits, methods for financing, and apparatus for administration, today's patchwork of bilateral relationships (even those within the European convention framework) is hardly surprising. The result for migrants or potential migrants, however, is a bewildering variety of coverages and gaps, rights and eligibilities matched with denials of benefits and losses of rights. Formal and informal barriers in obtaining social security supports in the post-migration living situation surely inhibit migration and thereby restrict the ability of workers to participate in and take advantage of the opening of world markets. Bilateral or multilateral legal arrangements devised for ensuring the financial integrity of the different national systems or for enhancing their administrative convenience do not necessarily suffice to encourage migrants to comprehend and exercise their rights.

Indeed, these barriers undoubtedly contribute to the characteristic phenomena of contemporary migration: that migrants tend overwhelmingly to be poor or rich, rather than from the broad middle spectrum of the occupational distribution; and that many migrants tend not to qualify for certain social security benefits. At the bottom end of the jobs ladder, poorer migrants find the prospect of immediate economic betterment through higher wages to be primary; the anticipated loss of social security protections due to a move may seem secondary. At the top of the jobs ladder, highly qualified migrants, such as managers, professionals, and scientific personnel, can afford private systems of insurance, medical care, and other social security supports in place of socially provided benefits. Those who are typically missing in this migration picture are the broad middle layers, for whom social supports constitute an important, even crucial element in the family's normal consumption pattern, and for whom the loss of (or uncertainty about) social security is sufficient to inhibit migration entirely.

This biased or incomplete representation of migrants also results in the often-noted pattern of migrants not establishing their eligibility for social security, even in circumstances where they may (compulsorily) be making contributory payments in support of the system. Poor migrants may be blocked by the informal barriers; high-level job seekers may simply choose private alternatives.

In considering positive policy changes that would ensure migrants their rights and encourage workers to take advantage of emerging cross-national employment opportunities, the various ILO conventions have surely pointed the way to important first principles. Equality of treatment between nationals and non-nationals, applicability of one legislation only, maintenance of acquired rights and of rights in the course of acquisition, and payment of benefits to eligible recipients residing abroad are important standards that should characterize any internationally accepted system.

The ILO standards fall far short, however, of a program of effective affirmative actions to guarantee migrants their rights and to assist potential migrants in acquiring adequate knowledge about and evaluating their likely eligibilities for social security. Such a program would include at least the following:

1. Assigning the responsibility for adjustment (for example, for enrollment and certification of eligibility) to

the social agencies rather than placing it on the migrant. This first new element underlies all the others: it would shift the burden of action from the migrant to the relevant national social agency. The point is simple: rather than assuming that it is up to the migrant's initiative to satisfy all of the procedural stipulations and documentary requirements to establish eligibility, it ought to be the social agency's obligation to assist the migrant and in general take as its responsibility the process of enrolling the migrant in the social security system. This may involve devoting special personnel only to this task, so that such administrators will themselves become familiar with the rules and administrative procedures relevant to (and even be fluent in the language of) the migrant.

2. Provision of comprehensive information. Each of the participating states (for example, the OECD countries) should provide, in one convenient packet, relevant and complete information on the availability of benefits in each of the social security branches, including all requirements for establishing eligibility, probationary periods, and so forth. Such information should be written in layman's language understandable to the ordinary person rather than in the bureaucratic language of social agencies. Such packets should be available in translated form in the languages of the reciprocal participating states and obtainable in the country of origin of a potential migrant.[9]

3. Provision of accepted documentation. A potential migrant ought to be able to obtain, before migrating, full and complete documentation required to establish credentials for social security enrollment. This document should serve as a social security "passport," providing entry into the social welfare network of the recipient country, much like an ordinary passport serves to establish the traveler's identity for the border guards.

4. Cross-national linkage of social security files. For citizens of participating states who so request, the social security files should be able to be linked cross-nationally to provide accurate information and record-keeping (for example, so that health providers may have access to relevant medical records, workers may be guaranteed that they will be properly credited with work history, contributory payments and other elements necessary to qualify them for old-age pensions, and so on). Cross-national linking of files undeniably raises concerns about civil liberties and privacy, and would therefore have to be carefully constrained by binding and effective regulations to ensure that such files would be available only for legitimate social security business. But the enormous advantage for a migrant is assurance that his or her profile is not "lost" from bureaucratic sight.

Notes

1. David Marsden and Paul Ryan, "The Transferability of Skills and the Mobility of Skilled Workers in the European Community," *PerItaca Report* (PerItaca: Rome, 1990); *Labour Market Flexibility: the Current Debate* (Dahrendorf Report), Report of a High Group of Experts (OECD: Paris, 1986); G. Standing, *Unemployment and Labour Market Flexibility: SWEDEN* (ILO: Geneva, 1988).

2. See for instance Paul Butcher and Joseph Erdos, "International Social Security Agreements: The U.S. Experience," *Social Security Bulletin*, vol. 51, no. 9 (September 1988), pp. 4–13; Potito Di Nunzio, "Il Trattamento Fiscale per i Lavoratori all'Estero," *Diritto & Pratica del Lavoro*, no. 10 (1985), pp. 689–92; Sergio Grasselli, "Il Lavoro Italiano all'Estero," *Diritto & Pratica del Lavoro*, no. 41 (1986), pp. 2625–628; *I Lavoratori Stranieri in Italia* a cura di Giorgio Gaja (Il Mulino: Bologna, 1984). International Labor Conference, "Social Security Protection in Old-Age," General Survey of the Committee of Experts on the Application of Conventions and Recommendations, International Labor Conference, 76th Session (ILO: Geneva, 1989).

3. See Council of Europe, *Explanatory Reports on the European Convention on Social Security and on the Supplementary Agreement for the Application of the European Convention on Social Security* (Council of Europe: Strasbourg, 1973). C. Villars, "Social Security for Migrant Workers in the Framework of the Council of Europe," *International Labour Review*, vol. 120, no. 3 (May–June 1981), pp. 291–302. Other, narrower multilateral agreements include the Agreement on Social Security of Rhine Boatmen (1950), Nordic States Agreement (1955), and various trilateral arrangements. See International Labor Organization, "Liste des instruments internationaux de sécurité sociale" (ILO: Geneva, 1984).

4. Reliable data on the number of migrants living outside social security protection are lacking; however, the ILO, summing up the available research, notes "the failure of some benefits (particularly means-tested benefits), to reach their target groups has been shown to be substantial." International Labor Organization, *Into the Twenty-First Century: The Development of Social Security* (ILO: Geneva, 1984), p. 76.

5. See especially Conventions 118 (Convention Concerning Equality of Treatment of Nationals and Non-Nationals in Social Security) and 157 (Convention Concerning the Establishment of an International System for the Maintenance of Rights in Social Security); Helmut Creutz, "The I.L.O. and Social Security for Foreign and Migrant Workers," *International Labour Review*, vol. 97, no. 4 (April 1968). See also International Labor Conference, *Maintenance of Migrant Workers' Rights in Social Security*, (Revision of Convention 48), International Labor Conference, 67th Session, Report VII(i) (International Labor Organization: Geneva, 1981); OECD, *Reforming Public Pensions*, Social Policy Studies No. 5 (OECD: Paris, 1988).

6. Convention 118, Article 3; International Labor Organization, *Social Security for Migrant Workers* (ILO: Geneva, 1977).

7. By 1989 only Spain and Sweden had ratified Convention 157; information furnished by the ILO.

8. This recommendation parallels an ILO finding: "Social Security has grown to a vast size without developing an adequate public information and public education service commensurate with its magnitude." ILO, *Into the Twenty-First Century* (op. cit), p. 74; see also p. 78, OECD, *The Future of Social Protection*, Social Security Studies, No. 6 (OECD: Paris, 1988).

9. In the United States, this simple-language requirement has been used effectively by various states in (e.g.) rules for insurance policies.

4

Encouraging Diverse Employments

THERE IS A SECOND AREA of opportunities and risks for
labor in the process of international economic integration:
the impact of this process on the diversity of employments
available to workers. Will integration open new possibilities and work to enrich the types of employment available
to workers? Or by contrast, will integration collapse the
range of existing employments, thereby presenting workers with an impoverished set of work-life options? And
how will international policy influence these outcomes?

We have already in part considered these questions by
arguing that international policy should work to extend
workers' geographic employment rights. But what about
the nonmigrating workers? Are they going to be affected
by the increased economic integration, and if so, how can
this process also produce beneficial outcomes for them?

In this chapter we argue that workers have a positive
interest in having available to them a diverse range of
employments, and that international policy can and should
attempt to encourage diverse employments and sustain
workers in their efforts to maintain, promote, and cross-

fertilize identities based on regional, occupational, cultural, linguistic, and other loyalties.

Labor's Stake in Diversity

How will nonmigrating workers be affected by the emerging processes of integration? This question is relevant, because even though there is great scope for appropriate policies to promote larger flows of international migrants, and even though ensuring skill transferability would imply that virtually all workers could share in the prospect and promise of mobility, ultimately the numbers of people actually involved in international migration will most likely be sharply limited. If the developed countries were to eliminate all formal and informal barriers to transnational labor mobility, one would still predict that only a minority of workers would move from one national market to another. What about the workers who remain?

The conventional point of view follows these lines: Workers, like other citizens, may be affected by the international economy in their roles as consumers, savers, taxpayers, and income receivers; more specific to workers, integration may influence the rates of employment and unemployment, both in the aggregate and by sector, and of course wage levels may be conditioned by international competition. But beyond those traditional dimensions of workers' interests, workers are seen as having little stake in integration, and in particular, workers as producers, that is, workers in their everyday lives at their workplaces, have little at issue in the question of international integration.

This point of view, we claim, is fundamentally wrong,

and derives from an overly narrow understanding of the interests of labor combined with a pedantic application of analogies taken from product and capital markets. It overlooks a possible loss that workers may suffer from integration, and it obscures an area where correct policy could produce beneficial outcomes for workers. It is, in short, another forgotten link.

The problem arises because labor is not recognized as a unique element in the economic matrix. A consumer, when enjoying some good, may be indifferent as to whether that good was produced abroad or at home. Whether it be made in Japan, in Europe, or in the United States, a car is a car, a steel coil is a steel coil, and a shovel is a shovel. The same is true of financial capital: *pecunia non olet*, the old dictum says. But labor is different. Labor always comes incorporated in people; and people live, work, and travel with their own culture, traditions, experiences, and abilities. Thus when growing economic integration causes change in the production and work lives of workers, its impact goes beyond the issues of unemployment and wage levels to the very quality and meaning of life itself.

It is often argued that the widening of a market has a broadly homogenizing effect. Market participants, who previously were isolated in local and parochial markets and thereby insulated from competition, are brought under the sway of a wider and shared competitive pressure. The result is that differences in goods or ways of producing are evened out, and standardized products and the "one best method" of production tend to prevail.

When this idea is applied to labor markets, the question becomes whether increasing integration will tend to standardize and thereby pauperize the range and diversity of employments available to workers, or will it support and enrich a more varied *mondo del lavoro*? It is a crucial question for labor.

We should note that increased migration could easily add to the pressures for standardization. Integration imparts momentum to the processes of standardization via the tendencies to standardize goods and to implement the one best method of production, but migration brings these pressures directly and immediately into the workplace. Migration affects the whole of the labor force, the stock of staying workers as well as the flow of migrants, the majorities as much as the minorities in the working population. All regions and all workers are affected by integrating labor markets, quite independently of the actual dimension and distribution of the migration flows, and this will affect social structures and institutions, educational and training systems, patterns of working time and leisure, production and technological mechanisms, market structures, and even traditions and habits.

Traditional ways of approaching the question of how to adapt to integration have until now been too constrained and prosaic. On one side it is conventional to pose the question of structural adaptation in terms of a single-country perspective rooted in the notion of a market-determined "best" outcome. The market is seen as a device for choosing the optimal arrangements (enterprise structure, organization of labor relations, and so on). Market competition may itself impose this "best" outcome, but for any individual country, its own policies can be used to assist and speed up the realization of conditions needed to achieve the hoped-for market outcome. Typically, the country's policy is then designed on the premise that it must adapt and conform to the leading country and its one "best" system. Debate turns to the choice of which country is the correct model, the institutional arrangements of the most successful national competitor being considered the best of all possible worlds. But underlying the debate is agreement that norms and rules have to be standardized, the standards being those provided by the "model" system and country. Integration would thus ultimately seem to require—according to this approach—the complete homogenization of skill structures and social systems at the global level as all systems converge on that of the leading country. This perspective, seen from the point of view of any local economy, and of the workers whose habits, roots, and needs are deeply integrated within the local culture, appears quite frightening, no less worrying from labor's vantage point than that of being completely left out of international economic integration. In fact it amounts to nothing less than a form of neoimperialism, whereby one country and one system impose its own rules of labor-market organization and of social stratification on the rest of the world.

On the other side, and equally frightening, is a perspective that we might call "technocratic structuralism." According to this perspective, no real country is taken to be the ideal, but rather a model system is constructed out of an eclectic combination of features borrowed from real cases, taken out of their historical and institutional context, and placed in some idealized design of optimal social structure and labor-market organization. We could have, let us say, a combination of the German training system, the Swedish labor-market organization, the Japanese firm structure, the Anglo-American system of research and educational institutions, and finally (why not?) the Italian informal economy. It would take a hyper-rationalist faith and a Bolshevik-style intervention to expect that such a system, however carefully designed by intellectuals, rigorously modeled by social scientists, and diligently adapted by administrators, could work better than any individual real system. It is indeed doubtful that it would even "work" at all.

It matters not whether "standardization" is induced by survival-of-the-fittest market pressures assisted by country policies modeled on the strongest and most advanced countries, or whether it is effected by the idealistic "Terror" of the international bureaucracies attempting to impose technocratic structuralism: local cultures and labor systems appear doomed to be wiped away by the integration wave. The allegedly superior "model" culture will see to the displacement and the destruction of the autonomous systems and norms.[1]

It is exactly the fear of such a daunting fate that justifies the lack of interest, or sometimes even the open opposition, of local communities to international integration. It is by now a well-established argument that product-market and capital-market integration is likely to put at risk the economic survival of the weakest local production structures. But the benefits expected from an integrated market, in terms of availability of goods, efficiency, productivity, and incomes and living standards, are such that most agree that it would be unwise to avoid those risks by maintaining protectionist barriers and that policy interventions can be devised to balance and compensate for the likely damages of increased economic integration.

But a lot more is at stake when integration comes to labor markets. Placed at risk are the social norms and values, the sense of identification with a community, the institutional mechanisms developed throughout centuries of common history, the whole culture of workers' lives and human relations. To wipe all this away for greater efficiency is a very steep price. No compensation would seem sufficient to justify the destruction of the local communities and the disposal of the immense variety of institutional systems that make local life richly distinct and interesting.

But is there an alternative to the homogenizing, standardizing imperatives of integration? Is the "normalization" of the local cultures a necessary condition for participating in the wider economic community? Is the standardization of labor-market rules and practices an ineluctable requirement of internationalization? We would claim that this is not the case.

It is, on the contrary, only owing to the "forgotten link" that technocratic structuralism or its market-driven single-country-model alternatives look inevitable. Neglecting labor's stake in the international economy and labor's roots in the richness and variety of local cultures promotes the common attitude that a massification of social practices is inevitable. It narrows the focus so that there appears to be a technical imperative to do away with local differences and to eliminate disparate institutions, social variations that are considered nothing more than useless complications. On the contrary, by putting labor and labor markets at the core of the internationalization of the economy, labor's stake in maintaining or even increasing the variety and richness of local cultures appears quite clearly.

Indeed, the argument against standardization applies more broadly than just to labor markets. The integration of goods markets and capital markets has also put pressure on firms, institutions, market structures, and government policies to "conform," and so the institutions and cultures of labor markets and labor processes are not the only ones at risk. A similar case can be made for technological choice, the pattern of government intervention, the structure of financial institutions, and so on. In those cases, as in the case of labor markets, the argument follows a similar line: While integration forces firms to perform, performance does not necessarily require conformity to a unique "best practice." There are many paths by which firms and nations might succeed.[2]

Much more research is needed in this field, and when we come to labor markets, the analysis of the relationship between integration and harmonization has not yet even started. Yet the lesson would appear to be similar: the labor process may be organized in many ways and still be efficient, and similar technologies are often consistent with different organizational structures; integration and standardization need not always go hand in hand. Clearly, from a labor perspective, there should be great emphasis placed on putting this question into the research and policy agenda.

The interests of the world of labor would seem to lie not in the standardization and unification of labor-market rules and practices on the grounds of nationalism, ideology or technological determinism. On the contrary, labor's stake is in respecting and giving full value to diversity, promoting the equal dignity of all local cultures, achieving the full "harmonization" of workers' ideals and institutions. Harmony does not in fact emerge from a single tune; rather, it requires a variety of themes and patterns, and the more elaborated the variety, the richer and more effective the impact of the ensemble can be.

Diversity and equal dignity—these are the values at stake

for labor and these are the desired properties of international economic integration. It is worth noting that the promotion of diversity does not represent a purely conservative stance, even if the preservation of the institutional and cultural environment is at least as important as that of the natural environment. People aim at giving value and strength to their cultures and traditions by exposing them on the basis of equal dignity to other cultures and traditions. Appropriate policy therefore need not be a static and passive defense, but rather could be an active promotion of and challenge to interaction and mixture with other cultures.

Diversity poses policy tasks that are at the same time pervasive and demanding but also relatively attainable. It implies the acceptance and enforcement of the principle that all local systems and local cultures should be allowed to coexist and interact on an equal footing. It involves demoting the forms of integralism and diminishing intolerance. It requires the adoption of the "culture of diversity" and its application to labor-market regulation and employment practices. But the failure to adopt the culture of diversity (and to assign a driving role to local economies in the promotion of integration) will itself be costly. It will produce either no effective and balanced integration (implying loss of potential welfare and impediments to the integration of capital and product markets) or the submission and destruction of many local labor civilizations, with the likely accompaniment of tensions and conflicts.

The current and potential development of technology could ensure, in our view, the practical feasibility of this formidable task. Effective translation systems have allowed different languages and literatures to coexist and interact. Widespread communication networks have made it possi-

ble to link up people, production processes, and institutions, overcoming geographic distances and technical barriers. Sophisticated software systems have connected and
jointly operationalized different machines and technical
equipments. New technological developments promise
such aids as, for example, telephones that simultaneously
translate, permitting people of different languages to com-
municate directly. Whole industries based on connectors,
adaptors, translators, converters, and transformers are
flourishing, while bureaucrats languish and quarrel over
uniform standards.

These developments constitute paradigmatic signals of
the great potentials that technology offers to allow diversity to exist, to promote the enrichment of cultural inter-
actions, and to foster the development of the local labor
markets. Technology, in order to respond to those vital
labor interests, must be directed toward developing social
and institutional communication mechanisms, and creating the appropriate "cultural software" that is required by
the promotion of diverse employment patterns in an internationally integrated labor market.

But the main preconditions for diversities to coexist are
"cultural" and in broad terms "political." The "culture of
diversity" must be adopted by all parts of the community.
Perhaps most importantly, it must be adopted by the
workers themselves, and by their official representatives in
the unions and labor parties. After all, labor's versions of
the "uniform standards ideology" also exist, and they
could prove difficult to uproot: for instance, the idea that
there is only one best system of protection of workers'
interests, and that all others are inferior and less effective.
Labor movements have sometimes gotten locked into
thinking that there is only one road that can be labor's

road, and all issues can be reduced to the question of how far down that road labor has progressed or can progress. This linear view of workers' protection is often the dominant one, especially in countries like Germany and Britain that have glorious traditions of labor movement achievements. But labor history in the last few decades has shown that there can be many roads to travel, different systems of protecting labor interests and of responding to labor demands. These systems grow out of the different institutions, cultures, and traditions of the labor movements in different countries, and remain deeply rooted in those particular labor histories. Analytically, this argument can be considered symmetrical to that of labor flexibility: as there is not a unique "model" of labor-market flexibility, but each successful system has developed its own formula and mechanism, so there is not a unique way of promoting workers' interests.[3] Accepting the diversities implies letting workers develop their own system of protection, by themselves, on the basis of their traditions, culture, and institutions.

The integration of labor markets should not force the convergence of different labor strategies in the search of the one best standard model of protection. On the contrary, it should promote the furtherance and development of diversified workers' protection mechanisms, systems that coexist not so much on the basis of competition due to different levels of protection but rather complement each other by diverse means and strategies to achieve comparable levels of protection.

The Dilemma of "Social Europe"

The discussions and policy confrontations that are going on in Europe in relation to the objectives of the Single

Market show clearly the complexities and the risks involved in taking into account the social dimension and the labor-market issues of transnational economic integration. As stated in the official declaration of the Hannover meeting of the EC Council of Ministers (June 1988), there is widespread consensus in Europe that "the consideration of the social dimension of the internal market represents a decisive condition for the successful achievement of the latter." In this framework, the Commission of the European Community developed a series of proposals and policy initiatives aimed at focusing and implementing the social dimension, that is, the idea of a "Social Europe."[4] In particular, the main lines around which European discussion and experimentation has occurred are the following:

1. The development of structural policies aimed at strengthening regional cohesion in Europe;

2. The creation of a legal statute of company regulation at the European level which foresees the participation of workers;

3. The establishment of a European charter of workers' rights;

4. The development of a widespread and effective "social dialogue," involving the main employees' and employers' organizations;

5. The harmonization at the highest possible levels of the conditions of health, safety, and hygiene at the place of work.

Other proposals have been formulated in a report prepared by the Commission on the "social dimension of the internal market," which was adopted in September 1988.[5] Member states' governments, the social partners, institutions, organizations, and regional and local communities have also been involved in discussions concerning the design and implementation of appropriate policy measures to accompany the realization of the Single Market. While very few policy-makers and commentators would question the need for Social Europe, there are quite considerable divisions and conflicts on the issue of which constitute the best policies to realize it. This has meant that progress has been slow and uncertain on all the issues concerning the so-called "social dimension." The Single Market is likely to show very little sign of Social Europe.

The policy deadlock can be interpreted in a schematic way as an unresolved clash between two equally persuasive and rooted, but opposite, approaches. On one side, there is the view that the systems and regulations that have proved successful in the most advanced European countries should be extended to all workers throughout the Community. This involves giving the European institutions great power to identify the best standards and practices, to evaluate the necessary adaptations and flexibilities to be allowed, and to implement the policy adjustments required both at the European Community level and at the level of individual countries.

This approach can be called "harmonization from above." It adopts a proactive European policy perspective, and it proposes directives, legislated norms, and central regulations that are immediately applicable throughout the Community or that need to be incorporated into national legislations. This approach is in general supported by the progressive pro-European movements of continental Europe (especially in France and Germany), and has as its champion the president of the EC Commission, the Socialist Jacques Delors.

On the opposite side, we find the view that national

institutions and practices should be defended, including the well-established national systems of workers' protection and the democratic mechanisms through which the organized representatives of labor have acquired some power and control over the political process. This approach is suspicious of and rejects all political interference by supranational institutions, and defends all the specificities and the features of national social and educational structures. It leaves to the market the task of singling out the best practice, and to that purpose it favors the competition of different national regulations. It has promoted the adoption of the principle of "mutual recognition," whereby different regulatory mechanisms are formally recognized everywhere throughout the European Community, leaving to the individual operators the freedom to adopt one or the other.

Thus, at one extreme, it is feared that the imposition of a unique model of social and labor-market regulation, *the* social dimension predicated by Brussels, is going to rigidify social and labor relations, preventing people (including workers) from doing what they think is best for themselves, producing an overly legislated hyper-regulation of labor practices, and creating obstacles and institutional impediments for the flexible functioning of the market. At the other extreme, it is claimed that without supranational regulation there will never be a social dimension to the Single Market at all. It is argued that it is reductive and one-sided to consider Europe simply as a "marketplace" rather than as a social and political "community." Moreover, it is feared that leaving the harmonization of the institutional structures to the market will imply deregulation, loss of workers' bargaining power and protection, impoverishment of the weaker national labor markets, and lack of solidarity.

Both poles of the Social Europe policy impasse appear persuasively odious and at the same time respectable: technocratic centralism opposed to nationalistic conservativism, bureaucratic oppression opposed to the market mechanism's "law of the jungle." Equally odious in prospective appears any compromise or mediation achieved through intergovernmental negotiation or Brussels-level "social dialogue" resulting in a little bit of both evils.

We claim that the deadlock on Social Europe can be attributed to the lack of a full understanding of labor's positive stake in labor-market integration and to the hidden "technocratic structuralism" of both the approaches discussed above. The "diversity argument" formulated herein allows us to go beyond the impasse. It requires in fact a proactive and interventionist policy in support of the social integration of labor in the European market economy, but a policy that at the same time would promote coexistence and interaction on the basis of the equal dignity of the diverse national and regional systems. Such a policy would need in particular to help the weaker labor segments and areas to develop at the international level.

The discussion so far allows us to make some progress toward answering the questions posed at the beginning of this chapter: Will integration open new possibilities and enrich the employments available to workers, or will it collapse and impoverish the existing range of work-life options? What is at stake for nonmigrant labor in the processes of international integration? The answers at this stage cannot be conclusive and, as is inevitably the case when new research perspectives are developed, they lead to further questions; yet at least an initial answer would be as follows.

As has been well known, there are two principal concerns that have been addressed in the scholarly literature. First, there is an *efficiency dimension* toward which labor is not and cannot be indifferent. If a more effective labor process leads to higher growth and employment, higher incomes, wages, and material standards of living, the labor interest is potentially great. Second, there is also an *equity and distributional dimension* to integration that is of great significance to labor: Labor will benefit from increased integration if (and only if) labor's positions in the social structure—its share in economic resources and its bargaining power in the collective dynamics—are not negatively affected by internationalization. Most policy discussions, including those initiated by the labor organizations, have dwelt at length on these two dimensions of the problem. Although they are far from being uncontroversial, we only touch upon them here to point out one at least arguable conclusion to that discussion, namely, that if appropriate policies are set in place, international economic integration can yield favorable outcomes to labor on both the efficiency and equity dimensions.

We add, however, a third dimension that is decisive to the identification of labor's positive stake in the internationalization of labor markets and labor processes, and this is the *diversity dimension.* Through international integration, workers may be exposed in their own labor markets to a variety of labor processes and conditions—diverse situations that could enrich their workplace choices and working life experiences as much as choice among consumer goods improves their living standards. But because labor-market integration across national boundaries inevitably amounts to a formidable process of social and institutional restructuring, it would be essential that these diverse work opportunities embody roughly equivalent levels of labor protection and bargaining power—essential, that is, if workers are to be actors in and initiators of social change and institutional innovation in the process of international integration of labor markets.

We would like to show that diversity in an integrated international labor market is not only desirable from the point of view of labor and society at large, but also that it is realistically achievable. But it will not happen by itself: it requires appropriate policies of active support. We will refer to these policies when we consider technology, regional development, and migrations.

If diversity, equal dignity, and the coexistence of different labor processes and cultures are encouraged, labor will experience and recognize positive gains in the opening up of labor markets. Workers will "demand" Japanese production methods just as they now demand Japanese cars (and which, like the cars, could be tailor-made for specific markets); they will "demand" German training systems as they now demand German machinery, and so on. International labor-market integration based on these principles could inject a positive change in how workers and society view the relationship that workers have with their own culture, institutions, and traditions. These sources of identity, rather than being perceived as "ties" or constraints, could come to be seen as "roots" or supports for a world of labor that workers have actively helped to cultivate.

Promoting Regional Diversity

The regional economy, with its localistic customs and practices and its peculiar traditions, represents one of the most significant sources of diversity and hence of identification for workers. Labor's stake in supporting and maintaining the local dimension of economic activity implies that careful consideration must be given to the impact that internationalizing the market will have on the position of the diverse local communities. Here, too, appropriate policies may promote positive outcomes.

What determines how a traditional regional economy will fare when exposed to the processes of international integration? The fate of a local economy or a regional labor market is ambiguous and difficult to predict, because successful integration seems to depend upon many factors. Traditionally, one can distinguish among demand, supply, and institutional factors. The first category includes the growth potential of the local economy; by that we mean the capacity to provide sufficient demand so as to sustain a sufficiently fast rate of noninflationary economic growth and accumulation. Divergences in the speed of growth of integrating economies and lack of correspondence of their cyclical phases have caused, and are causing, significant tensions in the international economy. International economic policy coordination has often aimed at evening out those divergences. However, regulating or fine-tuning the pace of growth in an open worldwide economic scenario has never constituted a necessary nor a sufficient condition for balanced integration of different regional economies. By appropriately adjusting in-flows and out-flows of goods and services, and allowing leads and lags in the international payments, different national economies can coexist in equilibrium with divergent rates and phases of economic growth. For instance, the structure of supply and demand in a country like Japan has allowed it to grow much more rapidly than the countries with whom it has trade relationships.

A second set of factors, related to both demand and supply, is equally decisive for the performance of a regional economy in the international market. These factors involve the structure of supply and demand, and in particular the export elasticities of demand and the indicators of net import penetration. One important indicator of the development and balanced integration in the international economy is the long-term "full employment external payments balance." This measure gauges the capacity of an economic system to satisfy its needs directly or through international trade, in terms of both consumption and investment, and to avail itself of the intermediate inputs that are required to sustain its desired rate of growth and accumulation. Other indicators, more oriented to comparing relative levels of prosperity, are more ambiguous to interpret in this context.[6] In determining whether a local economy gains or loses from international integration, the long-run external payments balance is useful to check whether the local economy is able to attract investment from outside, to find outlets for local production of goods and services in the international market, and to adapt its production system and the technologies of the labor process in such a way as to be able to compete with other systems in terms of costs and quality of output.

There are also more purely supply-side factors in successful integration. These include cost competitiveness and nonprice competition; the composition of output and the changes induced by international integration in the sectorial balances; the availability of production factors (labor, entrepreneurial talent, managerial expertise, technology, and capital); and the internal integration of the local productive system at the intersectoral or at the interfirm level. A local economy that has access to effective technologies, that specializes in sectors for which there is an increasing demand in the world market, that can rely on the availability of abundant labor and capital of the appropriate kind, where firms and sectors are sufficiently specialized and integrated in the local system: this is the supply-side picture of the successful regional economy.

Finally there are institutional, cultural, or environmental factors. These are often neglected, but they have a determining influence on the international performance of a local economy. The optimal functioning of the structure of supply and demand often depends on factors such as the competitive climate or "industrial atmosphere," as Alfred Marshall called it. For instance, the quality of the labor force depends on the performance of the educational and training systems. The capacity to innovate, in terms of both technological invention and economic application, is related to systems of research and development and to social mechanisms of access to entrepreneurship, of enterprise creation, of interaction between large and small or medium-sized firms. The dynamism of the social structure in terms of social mobility and turnover has a great impact on the flexibility of the labor market.

The listing of the relevant factors of performance in the international economy permits an accurate view of the anatomy of the successful local economy. However, the "physiology" of successful performance is a much more complicated matter. It is in fact difficult to describe how these factors combine and interact effectively in a systemic framework, and above all in a policy perspective, how intervention and support mechanisms can be designed and operationalized, taking appropriately into account the set of interrelated functions and relationships. Two important conclusions of a recent study by Carlo Borzaga and Raffaele Brancati are worth being highlighted in this context:

1. First of all, achieving strong regional economic performance does not depend on limiting the degree of openness of the local economy. Actually, looking at the experience of the 1980s in Italy, Borzaga and Brancati conclude that "the regional and provincial areas that are more open to trade exchanges are those that present a more favorable economic performance."[7] Therefore, all responses couched in terms of mere defense and protection of the local economy appear inappropriate: they lead to missing out on the great potential benefits that the integration of the local economy into a wider market and community can have and in general has had. Considering for instance the Italian Mezzogiorno, it is worth noticing not only that there is a persistent and significant trade deficit with the rest of the country and the rest of the world, but also that the size of the exposed sector is small and the level of trade exchanges is low in relation to those of the more developed areas of Northern Italy.

2. "The prevailing effects [of integration] on the local economies are uncertain and depend on a pluralism of different factors."[8] The main difficulty in developing reliable predictions is in the fact that the systemic elements prevail over the individual components of the successful performance. The existence in a regional economy of large conglomerates, aggressive in export markets, can certainly represent a comparative advantage, but success can also be achieved, and in fact has been achieved, in systems dominated by small and medium enterprises, as in Lyons or Baden-Würtemberg. Successful regional economies typically have small and effective public sectors, but some of them (for example, in Sweden and West Germany) have large and pervasive bureaucracies. Some regional economies specialize in high-tech sectors, others successfully

compete in traditional or mature industries. Sometimes we find a locality that has, at the root of its successful economic performance, low labor costs and flexibility based on unfavorable working conditions, whereas other successful areas have based their success on high pay, labor productivity, high standards of labor, and employment protection.

The conclusion is that there is not a single "model" of successful regional integration, but that many effective systems and economically efficient structures can be developed at the local level, structures that are different in different regions and in diverse institutional contexts. Evidently there is not a "single road" to successful performance in an open economy, but many possible paths exist. Thus, the diversity of local economies can be consistent with increasing international integration and the balanced opening of localistic barriers. Moreover, as our prior diversity argument would suggest, diversity is not only permissible and compatible, it is also desirable from labor's point of view. The exposure to different cultures has allowed, and even more could allow, labor to enjoy greater opportunities and freedom of choice within both the consumption and the production structures—that is, a wider basket of goods and production processes. But the precondition for reaping the benefits of diversity is the maintenance and promotion everywhere of local identities, cultures, and institutions, a task that implies the maintenance and promotion of local production systems and of regional labor market organizations.

This idea coincides with a reformulation in a wider and more comprehensive framework of the notion of "endogenous growth," now seen in a global perspective. For an individual economy, endogenous growth implies the development of those features and patterns in consumption, in production, and in the process of capital accumulation that correspond to the needs and aspirations of the local community. These features must become positive elements contributing to the effective functioning of the local economy. Endogenous growth also means developing those features "from within" and "from below," with deep and wide involvement of the local actors, the social partners, and the institutions of the local community.

However, endogenous growth applies to one individual economy, or better to any local economy taken separately, in isolation from all the others. It is not capable by itself of bringing into focus the forgotten link in international economic policy cooperation. And it is the forgotten link that has condemned labor to a defensive and passive role vis-à-vis the integration of local communities, for essentially two reasons.

First, "endogenous development" cannot be expected to take place everywhere and at the same extent by itself. There is not an effective decentralized market mechanism that ensures that all communities develop and progress in parallel due simply to the sheer elimination of the formal barriers and to the increased interconnectedness of the local economies. On the contrary, more often the lack of active support has implied that the weaker and more fragile local economies have been threatened by displacement and elimination. The market by itself can often be a threat to diversity, even though diversity enhances and stimulates the role of the market. Therefore endogenous development with diversity cannot be left to the exclusive responsibility and efforts of the local communities.

Second, the market and the no-interference postulate of much public policy have provided a pretext for carrying out policies of international integration that are based on the technocratic assumption that there is only "one road" to development, and that therefore diversity is a flaw or an impediment that has to be overcome by appropriate "standardization" policies. There is one best technology for each production process—it is alleged—and there is one best labor process and organization, one structure of competitive product and labor markets, one optimal government macroeconomic adjustment policy, and even one best social system and structure. Corresponding to this perspective, there is also only one best system of labor protection. There cannot then be—according to this view—more than one road to the development and the integration of the local economy. Only minor adjustments can be allowed at the local level to take into account local peculiarities and distortions, but even these come at the price of slowing down and reducing progress toward high performance.

This attitude, which we have termed technocratic structuralism, can have and has had devastating effects on local diversities. A misconceived opening up of local economies has often resulted in bringing about or accentuating decay and underdevelopment. This has shown up in structural balance of trade deficits and so further results in increasing dependency on external financial support. These deficits signal the inability to produce a viable and balanced consumption and production structure at the local level.

The displacement effects associated with the enforcement of integration from above appear even more clearly at the level of labor-market organization and institutional adjustment. The outcome of "structural standardization" has often been the impoverishment of the local culture, domination by external influences, and finally the loss of local identity and the sense of community.

This is not to deny that painful adjustments sometimes need to be made at the local level to accommodate to the crude realities of the changing market conditions. Nor does it imply that the local economy needs to be sheltered and protected from exposure to the potentially damaging trends and pressures of international competition. Neither policies that prevent the necessary adjustment, that can lead to loss of efficiency, and that negatively affect growth potential, nor laissez-faire policies that passively accept the decay and the disruption of the local economy are likely to result in healthy integration of regional economies. Moreover, the latter policies cannot be justified even in the conventional terms of mainstream economics, because the efficiency gains thus realized take account of only the private-sector profits and costs, whereas the externalities and social costs involved in dislocations are neglected.

These negative consequences, the plight of underdevelopment, decay, and poverty, affect not only labor but the whole of the local community. They are generally perceived and acknowledged, particularly by unions and political constituencies, and have therefore effectively stimulated a growing demand for economic growth and regional policies and an active policy for development. However, it is the world of labor that can relate these effects most strongly and coherently to the determining factors of an "integralist" integration. And it is the world of labor that can most acutely perceive, appreciate, and experience the fundamental value of diversity, because workers necessarily have their roots so deeply in the local cultures and institutions.

Ironically, to achieve not only the protection and maintenance but also the promotion and integration of local diversities, labor has to assume an international perspective. By remaining confined within the myopic boundaries of localism and localistic defense, labor has often provided an alibi to, or even played the role of the unaware ally of, the approach of integration from above.

In conclusion, internationalization of the regional economies can have ambiguous effects on the local communities. In general it can be said that integrating the local economies opens up vast new opportunities for labor in terms of living standards, working conditions, and private and public prosperity. But in order for those benefits and potentials to be realized it is necessary to devise accompanying measures at both the local and the international level. An active policy of local labor-market integration has to be based on the principle of promoting local diversities and of enhancing the variety and richness of local cultures, institutions, and traditions. This involves acting at the local level for developmental purposes, supporting the improvement of local production processes and methods, the local creation of new goods and services, research and experimentation of new technological processes on-the-spot and in close contact with the local business community, and the involvement of the local communities, local labor organizations, and local institutions in the design and implementation of international integration policies.

The local dimension must become a fundamental and predominant framework for policy action and support. But the local dimension must be perceived and evaluated in a global context, accepting and promoting the coexistence of different cultures and economic systems. This implies also that international efforts should be aimed at promoting labor-market integration by acting at the level of the weakest local economies. In this perspective, the support for the weakest does not simply represent a solidaristic response. Nor does it reflect simply the conventional point of view that the social dimension must compensate for and counteract the economic dimension of international integration. The local dimension is in fact above all a condition for the promotion of diversity in the world economy, one that enriches the development of the full potentials of international interaction among productive systems and social structures, one which is at once part of labor's stake in international economic cooperation but not only labor's.

Exploiting Technological Diversity

Technological innovation and change have played central roles in stimulating the emergence of an internationally integrated economy. The new technologies contain vast promise for sustaining diversity, for revivifying decentralized activities, and for creating new sources of varied employments. Yet they also contain manifold new risks for the world of labor. Thus labor has a significant stake in how these technologies take root in the economic process and in how the processes of integration work to produce beneficial outcomes. Will economic policy be implemented in a way that recognizes labor's concerns as well as the needs of other social partners?

Rapid technical change has driven the dynamism of the new economic relations both because it opened new economic (profit) possibilities and because the particular nature of the innovation has lent itself to development and application on an international scale. The first aspect is a relatively familiar one: New technologies are invented, making possible new products and the production of existing products in new ways. The new products and new production methods serve to displace prior products and methods, thereby creating a disequilibrium situation in which entrepreneurs or others can earn profits. The exploitation of this disequilibrium situation involves the successive application of the new techniques in different areas, different markets, different stages of production and consumption, and thus throughout the structure of economic relationships.

Technical change opens new economic possibilities and has historically provided the basis for growing productivity and incomes in all the developed countries. Although the process of implementing innovation contains many dislocations and adverse consequences as well, technological change, as Timothy Koechlin notes, "through its effect on productivity, is widely acknowledged as a critical path by which societies may increase their economic well being."[9]

Much of the innovation in the past decade or two, however, has also taken a specific form—the development of information technologies or IT—that has particular impact on the international integration of economic relations. Information technologies, meaning the related innovations in computers, artificial intelligence, robotics, telecommunications, controls, and other forms of information processing, make possible a level of coordination and integration vastly greater than was feasible even as recently as two decades ago. Thus the major economic actors, and in particular the multinational corporations, have discovered that both to defend themselves from aggressive competitors and to exploit new profit opportunities, they have been compelled to move quickly and decisively and with substantial force to internationalize and integrate their operations.

Technological innovation should be understood here to refer to an economic rather than a merely scientific phenomenon. The scientific process of discovery and invention produces a growing body of basic knowledge that is potentially at the disposal of economic agents to use. While the growth of this basic knowledge is undoubtedly affected by its economic consequences (for example, more resources will be made available to support research on matters where profitable results are anticipated), the growth of scientific knowledge is affected by many other factors as well. The economic process of the development, application, and implementation of new technologies is a parallel but largely independent activity, premised to be sure on the preexisting fund of basic knowledge but conditioned also by the expectations for profitable exploitation. For example, it is primarily an economic decision, not a scientific or technological one, that determines which of many scientific discoveries are taken up for commercial development, and when they are taken up, how quickly and extensively they will be pursued.

Technological innovation as an economic phenomenon is realized only through investment in new products, new machines, new organizations of production, or other measures that require investment. Thus the initial control over innovation, and specifically the decisions about which options within the range of technical possibilities to choose for development and whether to initiate the process of implementation of new technologies, remains almost exclusively in the hands of management.

To the extent that technology's impact is primarily a "private" one—that is, to the extent that all of the benefits and costs of technological diffusion can be captured by a productive enterprise—then private control over this process may be warranted and socially beneficial. Markets and profit incentives may provide the best practicable system for organizing diverse efforts to achieve innovation.[10] Clearly in certain cases the system of private incentives has led to very rapid innovation, followed by the diffusion of benefits to consumers. The development of information technologies is a significant example: innovation has been rapid, and consumers have greatly benefited, directly through the spread of personal computers, electronic mail, and other new consumer products or services, and indirectly (for example, in product prices and availability of services) through efficiencies deriving from the dramatic and steep declines in the cost of computation and information processing.

Yet in many cases the full effects of technological change are not captured by the "private" benefits and costs. The OECD's Sundqvist Report notes the important social dimension of technology and argues that "the wider environmental and societal issues involved with any new technology" must be considered. Timothy Koechlin cites such issues as "the quality of work life, the quality of the environment, the costs of adjusting to technological change, the maintenance of community, and the distribution of income."[11] In line with the discussion of the previous section, we may add the dimension of diversity and local identity to the "social" aspects of innovation. For all of these dimensions, a private employer's calculation of the costs and benefits of a new technology is not necessarily going to be adequate.

In some cases, social participation in the development and diffusion of technical innovation has come early in the process. For example, governments frequently subsidize or even directly undertake the research process leading to new technologies. This is particularly the case with basic research (those fundamental scientific investigations that lay the basis for particular applications). Public enterprises may be important initiators of technical development. In certain cases public monies may be used to develop particular technologies thought to be of special public benefit. In other cases unions, workers' cooperatives, or other workers' groups have developed and implemented specific new technologies.[12]

But mainly such public participation has been exceptional, and social regulation of technology, whether through public agencies, collectively bargained agreements between unions and employers, or other means, generally involves intervention toward the end of the process, after employers have already developed and decided to implement an innovation. Thus public participation and regulation generally treat with the consequences of innovation.

Labor clearly has an important stake in how and under what conditions the new technologies are implemented. As many observers have noted, the introduction of new technologies can have vast implications, both positive and negative, for the occupational health and safety of workers, the security of their employment, the extent of their employment opportunities, the importance or obsolescence of their skills, the meaningfulness of their jobs, and the environmental quality of their neighborhoods.

Labor's stake in the process of technical innovation is therefore a broad one. Effectively controlling the development and implementation of new technologies, however, is highly problematic. Consider labor's constraints: When labor does play a role, it is usually late in the innovation process. Labor must encourage technological innovation, because it is through such change that productivities (and consequently wages) advance. Labor must avoid setting too many limits, because employers often have access to other sites, including sites in other countries, at which to locate their operations. And yet labor must attempt to control the adverse effects accompanying innovation's diffusion.

Technological change intersects with the issue of diversity because technology at once represents one of the gravest threats to diversity and one of the most promising means of supporting diversity. It poses a threat because its use, especially the use of information technologies by the multinational corporations, goes furthest toward permitting the cross-national standardizing of production methods, work norms, and other aspects of work life.

But the new technologies also contain the promise of creating new opportunities for small and medium-sized business and for enterprises using diverse and particularistic production methods. Information technologies make it possible for such enterprises to be connected with faraway markets for inputs and for them to find distant customers. They can work in parallel with similarly situated firms elsewhere, benefit from flexible specialization and market niches, and expand their markets even as large enterprises increasingly encroach upon their traditional, local markets. Thus, the new technologies may greatly assist in the maintenance of regional and other forms of diversity.

These considerations lead to three conclusions concerning international policy on technology:

1. Those international bodies that have influence on the development and implementation of technological change

must take into account the broader "public" dimensions of technology's impact and encourage those forms of technological diffusion that best address these wider concerns. As technology's impact spreads across national boundaries, the traditional mechanisms for governing and shaping its diffusion—mechanisms such as national trade union bargaining and national technology policy—are likely to become less effective as increasing integration undermines all forms of national regulation.

2. Labor needs to be provided with specific mechanisms of participation in the decisions to develop and implement new productive technologies. In many cases, as Timothy Koechlin points out, such participation has already been introduced by employers as a means of improving the impact (even in profit terms) of new technology. Such efforts need to be expanded.

3. Technology policy should encourage those developments of new technologies and assist in creating those means of utilizing new technologies that promote and encourage the survival and maintenance of regional diversity, local control, and community identities. Even as corporate development of technology tends for natural reasons to run toward technologies that standardize and unify separate regional markets and diverse national productive systems, the burden on public policy is all the greater to encourage development of the other potentials in the new technologies.[13]

The public responsibility for fostering technologies that support regional and other forms of diversity seems especially strong in the area of information technologies. As Koechlin notes, these technologies are important not only for their direct applications but also for their potential to provide a whole framework for all technologies. Comparisons to the coming of the railroads and the spread of electricity are not overdrawn. But those comparisons to "epoch-making" innovations go further. In the cases of both the railroads and electricity, extensive public investments were made to ensure that the benefits of the new technologies were available to most regions and sections of society, not just those areas that would be served by facilities built through the private market. In both Europe and the United States, railroad construction was heavily subsidized or directly undertaken by the state, and it included extensions to areas not (yet) deemed profitable by private interests. The same approach was used with electricity. In one of the most famous cases, electricity was brought to vast American farm areas through the Rural Electrification Administration of President Franklin Roosevelt's New Deal program; this project was a direct, and successful, contribution to making regional economies viable.

In the area of information technologies, a similar public intervention could be useful, in order to ensure that regional economies and other sources of diversity are supported by having effective access to this new technology. Moreover, information technologies appear to be consistent with a broad array of efficient organizational structures, but effective access might require special attention to the applications of IT, to render them appropriate for small enterprises and allow for regional and cultural differences. In this and other ways, public intervention could play a proactive rather than simply defensive role.

Notes

1. It is exactly the evidence they inadvertently produce for the possibility of maintaining local diversity within the integration of

national economies, and not an alleged new "second wave" of industrial standardization (albeit in the form of "flexible specialization") that we find most interesting in the work of Michael Piore and Charles Sabel, *The Second Industrial Divide* (Basic Books: New York, 1984).

2. The existing literature and evidence provide ample support to the diversity argument when applied to product markets: the debate on flexibility has shown that there are many ways of achieving it. See OECD, 1988 and 1989. The literature on technological innovation and diffusion has indicated the wide-ranging implications of structural adjustment and change; the evidence of increased trade flows among industrialized countries has pointed out the greater importance of intraindustrial rather than interindustrial trade, and therefore the pressures toward harmonization rather than specialization of industrial structures. See OECD, *New Technologies in the 1990's, A Socio-Economic Strategy* (Sundqvist Report), Report of a High Group of Experts (OECD: Paris, 1988). This literature has also highlighted the *policy conditions* that are required to ensure that integration does not endanger diversity and flexibility in the adjustment patterns of different countries.

3. For one exposition along these lines, see Richard Edwards, *Rights at Work: New Public Policy Strategies towards Workplace Rights* (forthcoming).

4. Statement of the Council of Ministers, European Community, Hannover, June 1988; see sources cited in Chapter 1, note 5.

5. Commission of the European Communities (Marin Report).

6. Particularly difficult to interpret in this context are those indicators that focus on the quantitative levels or the rates of growth of economic variables such as income, income per capita, and consumption. For example, it would be misleading to compare the relative underdevelopment of poor countries in those terms. There are certain local communities (take, for instance, Tyrol or an industrial district of central Italy), whose economy is so well integrated, solid, and effective that it looks (and most probably is) much more prosperous and developed in terms of welfare and standards of living than richer areas that appear congested, prone to conflicts, divided and disorderly.

7. Carlo Borzaga and Raffaele Brancati, "L'impatto della Cooperazione Economica Internazionale sulle Economie Locali," *PerItaca Report*, p. 4.

8. Borzaga and Brancati, "L'impatto della Cooperazione," p. 10; R. Plant, *Industries in Trouble* (ILO: Geneva, 1981).

9. Timothy Koechlin, "Labor, Technological Change, and International Economic Integration," *PerItaca Report*, p. 1; also see sources cited therein.

10. Even here there are reasons for concern about the "internal" externalities of innovation driven purely by profit considerations. For example, the range of job opportunities offered to workers may be artificially restricted, compared to what would exist if workers or an external (e.g., public) agent were involved; while these effects may remain within the scope of the firm, they nonetheless mark a discrepancy between profitable and efficient development of technology. See for example R. Edwards and S. Bowles, *Understanding Capitalism* (Harper and Row: New York, 1985), Chapter 9.

11. OECD, 1988 (Sundqvist Report), p. 13. T. Koechlin, "Labor, Technological Change," p. 6.

12. Koechlin, "Labor, Technological Change."

13. Koechlin, "Labor, Technological Change," provides persuasive evidence and arguments to support this issue.

5

Managing South–North and East–West Migrations

SO FAR WE HAVE CONSIDERED some aspects of labor's interests in the nature of the economic integration emerging within the world of the advanced industrial democracies. But labor also has a stake in the form of those economic relationships being forged, during the processes of integration, with the rest of the world.

Increasing integration and development within the First World has been accompanied by increasingly close economic ties between it and the Third World, and certainly the transformations in Eastern Europe will bring vastly expanded economic relations between the First World and Eastern Europe. In part these ties have taken and will take the form of growing trade flows between the various regions. Another part has involved and will continue to involve the outflow of capital from the First World to be invested in the less developed regions of the world.

But there is still a third form that these growing ties have taken and will take: the migration of large numbers of workers *to* the First World. Already a vast stream of unskilled laborers has flowed from the underdeveloped nations ("the South") to the developed nations of Western Europe and North America ("the North").[1] And we can anticipate the possible opening of a second stream of workers, this time from the Second World of the Soviet Union and Eastern Europe ("the East") toward the developed countries of "the West." This second flow, consisting of both unskilled and skilled workers, is likely to be significant under any circumstances, but it could become very large if the Eastern European governments are unable to quickly generate rapid economic growth.

Labor in the advanced countries has a significant stake in how these migrations are regulated and controlled. At one extreme, that of the gravest danger to indigenous labor, the pools of new labor could be utilized in a new class war against workers in the North and West. Migrating workers from South and East could so drastically expand labor supplies in the advanced countries as to reduce wages, erode working conditions, and threaten the viability of the workers' organizations. At the other extreme, entry could be so tightly regulated that, while it poses minimal dangers to existing workers' interests, they (and others) are denied the benefits that flow from infusing the advanced countries' labor markets with new talents and skills.

To what extent will international policy be rooted in an appreciation of the impact, for good or ill, that South–North and East–West migrations can have on the world of labor? That is, to what extent will policy recognize this forgotten link?

Coordinating South–North Migration

Particularly in the 1960s and early 1970s, the South–North migration played a significant role in filling the labor needs of the North during the long economic boom. More recently, however, this migration has assumed a somewhat different character. First, the demand for unskilled labor in the manufacturing and industrial sectors of the Northern economies has leveled off or declined, so the demand factor "pulling" such migrants has eroded and the prospects for such migrants, once they arrive in the North, have changed. Increasingly, human resource planners in the Northern countries worry about looming shortages in skilled rather than unskilled labor. In any event the Northern countries, among the unemployed, underemployed, and youth workers, have sources of excess unskilled labor already. Second, in the face of Northern countries' efforts to restrict immigration, illegal or clandestine migration continues to be a difficult problem. The American effort to reform its immigration policy by offering amnesty to long-resident illegals, establishing temporary work permits for certain agricultural laborers, and instituting tougher immigration controls has been widely accepted as only a very partial success. Similar concerns about the African migration into Italy and the wider problem of illegal entry into the European Community after the elimination of internal border controls in 1992 likewise point to intractable problems. Moreover, by some measures such migration is even increasing. Indeed, Makis Cavouriaris declares that "les années 90 seront la décennie des clandestins. . . ."[2] Thus the governments of the North may well be faced with growing problems of illegal immigration.

Given that there remain very large pools of excess labor in the countries of the South, and that the historical standards of wages and working conditions for the employment of this labor have been very low in comparison with the achieved standards in the countries of the North, the continued migration of labor from the South could directly threaten the maintenance of labor's living standards in the North. Thus labor in the North has a direct stake in the manner and extent of the North's admission of migrant labor from the South.

The connections among the various elements involved in South–North migration are in fact quite complex and subtle and not perfectly understood, and therefore straightforward conclusions are somewhat suspect. Among the connections are these: Labor from the South that directly competes with indigenous labor in the North is likely to have the usual market effects of reducing the bargaining power, and hence the wages and working conditions, of all those brought into such competition. On the other hand, ordinary observation and considerable anecdotal evidence suggest that despite high levels of unemployed and redundant labor in the North, many of the workers migrating from the South wind up in jobs that are not deemed acceptable by unemployed Northern labor. In this respect the Southern labor is not competitive with Northern labor, and Northern labor undoubtedly enjoys real benefits (as a complementary factor of production as well as consumers of what such Southern migrant labor produces) from the presence of Southern migrants. Further complicating the issue is the fact that labor shortage is frequently a powerful stimulus to innovation and increased investment per worker. Thus the availability of Southern migrant labor may serve to retard the development of new technologies and new investments that would effectively transform the relevant jobs so as to make them acceptable to the unemployed and redundant labor that had previously rejected such employment. Another complicating factor is that the possibility of capital mobility to the South means that if such capital is deprived of adequate low-wage labor in the North, it may move its operations, or such part of its operations as are relevant, to the South, thereby depriving labor in the North not only of the low-wage jobs but perhaps also the skilled and qualified employments and the taxes and other contributions to social supports that would have resulted had the capital remained in the North. Finally, to the extent that economic growth in the South is stimulated, labor in the North will find increased employment through the export of products to the South.[3]

South–North migration has everywhere in the North been regulated, as the developed nations have felt the need to insulate their institutions and protect various constituencies from too much migration. This regulation has been effected in two principal ways. One method is to restrict access to the national territory itself, by means of effective border controls, restrictive visa and work permit policies, and other measures to control the immigration flow. The second method is to regulate entry into the national labor market, by means of various formal and informal controls and segmentations that place migrant workers in a secondary position. Each country has adopted a distinct mix of these policies, sometimes changing its mix over time.

But trade unions and other constituencies have become more sensitive to and critical of the second, or segmentation, approach, especially as that approach builds upon formal or legal controls (for example, temporary work permits). Labor-market administrators have found it more difficult to sustain the double legal standards required to operate such a system, particularly as the system itself has come under increasing attack for its segmentations based on nationality, race, sex, age, and other personal attributes. Thus have governments turned increasingly to the first method, restriction of entry into the territory itself, as their policy of choice, and thus too have clandestine or illegal migrations become more prominent.

Regardless of the method pursued, such policies tend to be less successful in regulating migration the longer the duration of the migrant's stay. As Makis Cavouriaris notes in his recent study, there has been a certain convergence in the policies of most of the OECD countries concerning "intégration des migrants permanents."

Given these extremely complex patterns of economic interrelationships, one must be hesitant to state conclusively what is the interest of labor in the North with respect to such migration. Nonetheless, it can be said that the advantages derived by Northern labor, if any, from Southern migration come from that initial level of Southern migration that results in such migrants taking up employments not competitive with Northern labor; and that greater levels of Southern migration place such migrants increasingly in competition with indigenous Northern labor, to the latter's detriment. That is, Northern labor's benefit from in-migration derives from the extent to which migrant labor remains a complementary factor of production with Northern labor and does not become a substitutive factor. (Employment under conditions of competition may still be in the interest of the Southern migrants, given that they face a much poorer set of opportunities in the South.)

There are also, of course, the interests of Southern labor (as well as others' interests) to be considered. As Cavouriaris reminds us, for some migrants (political refugees, stateless persons, persons being reunited with family members, and so on), the opportunity for economic betterment through migration is only a secondary consideration. For most "economic" migrants, presumably the benefit from migration would be evaluated as no more than equal to, and in most cases probably inferior to, equivalent economic betterment were such betterment available in the "home" country. However, Southern migrants' opportunity for transnational mobility also has a moral claim, even if such mobility threatens the standards (or "privileges") of Northern labor. Labor's stake in international economic cooperation ought not be taken to imply that only Northern labor's interests are at stake and need to be considered.

Growing economic integration has not relieved the developed countries of their obligations to assist in the development of the Third World (and increasingly, the Second World as well). This assistance takes many forms— financial grants, direct investment, technical assistance, export and import preferences, and so on. Labor, as a social partner, shares in both the interest in and the obligation for such assistance.

Labor migration from the underdeveloped countries to the developed nations can also be seen as a form of development assistance. It is only necessary to consider the relation of worker remittances to exports to see the importance of this form of aid: for Pakistan, for example, in 1986 remittances amounted to 66.3 percent of total exports; also in 1986: for Morocco, 39.1 percent; for Yugoslavia, 24.3 percent; for Burkina Faso, 64.7 percent.[4] This source of foreign exchange thus represents a crucial means of financing needed imports. However, as was suggested above, migration as a form of aid can have unfavorable consequences for the interests of labor in the North and the South, and it is to those interests as a whole that one must look when choosing an optimal migration policy.

This line of argument would suggest that migration has to be considered in connection with other forms of assistance (financial aid, direct investment) that might appropriately substitute or complement, for these migrants, for the opportunity to migrate. There should in fact be a limit to the role that economic incentives to migration play in the structural adjustment, this limit being some form of "worldwide safety net" that only world economic development can bring about. Moreover, the unregulated opening up of a national labor market to foreign labor risks becoming an exercise in universalistic rhetoric if the receiving economies do not have the resources and are not prepared to invest them in order to provide immigrants with jobs, public services, and opportunities for a decent life on an equal footing with native workers. Therefore, if on one side Northern labor cannot afford to be insensitive to the demands of Southern labor, on the other it cannot assume there will be no price to pay for labor's generosity and international solidarity.

These various considerations lead us to the following conclusions:

1. Some South–North migration is, with a high degree of probability, in the interests of Northern labor, and with an even higher degree of probability is not detrimental to Northern labor. Moreover, this migration undoubtedly has substantial benefits for (Northern) society in general and for the Southern migrants as well as benefiting, as we

have seen, the nations of the South by providing them with an important source of foreign exchange in the form of remittances.

2. There is, however, a point at which South–North migration begins to change the situation in the labor markets of the North from a positive-sum game (where all social partners share benefits) to a zero-sum game (where the benefits to some come at the expense of losses to others). In particular, such migration may produce benefits for migrants, who gain access to better jobs, and for employers in the national labor market as a whole, who gain access to a more competitive and adaptable labor force, but these gains come at the expense of some segments of Northern labor, who experience increased competition and loss of privileges and compensation. Northern labor should not in this case assume it has the right to push for establishing barriers to limit access from outside in order to protect its own national or sectional interests. Rather, it needs to take a broader international view, but above all, it needs to do what it can to integrate immigrants into the social, political, and industrial relations structures of the national labor market. Regulatory policy should aim at precisely that: providing the conditions for an acceptable insertion and full integration of immigrant workers into the economy. Limitations to entry should be resorted to only when the economic and financial constraints and other costs that such integration entails preclude adequate integration of further migrants.

3. South–North migration might become so extensive and unregulated that only employers would gain from it, as it would force the competitive pressures in the labor market to excessive levels, drive working and living conditions of immigrants in secondary labor markets to un-

acceptable standards, and threaten the material living standards and established working conditions of indigenous labor. This is the case where migrations should be constrained and limited, and other mechanisms of aid should be sought to fulfill the obligation to assist the less developed world to achieve economic growth. Earlier we argued with respect to transnational mobility that Northern labor should be allowed to migrate; here we argue that Southern labor should not be forced to migrate.

4. The extensive South–North illegal or clandestine migration needs to be acknowledged and addressed, in both its causes and its consequences, by the nations of the North. Its primary cause seems simple: there is an economically beneficial transaction possible in such migration, beneficial both to the migrant and to the (Northern) employer of the migrant or user of the migrant's services. As with the effort to prohibit other economically profitable transactions (for example, drugs, weapons, prostitution), more severe enforcement by itself is unlikely to constitute an adequate answer. As to its consequences, it has been widely recognized (though too little acted upon) that the illegality of such migration produces damage to the migrant, who is thereby placed under a burden of not being able to exercise any occupational, civil, or other rights for fear of discovery and deportation. What has not been sufficiently recognized is that the pervasive reality of such migration also damages the host country, by creating a domestic population outside the normal channels of the law and of community life, with little commitment to or stake in the host society.

Both of the conventional approaches to this migration thus appear flawed. On the one side, we see efforts to increase border security to stop the flow of illegal migrants. But given the economic rewards available to migrants from successful migration, it appears unlikely that such efforts, at least within the range of enforcement strategies normally associated with the Western democracies, will suffice. The other strategy, perhaps best typified by the Scandinavian countries, is to undertake extensive programs to integrate migrants into civil society, even to the extent of providing suffrage and other citizen's rights. But this policy implies an implicit restriction as well, since politically feasible support for such programs seems likely to fall well short of the level required to address the entire potential illegal migration.

In place of the conventional answers, a frank acknowledgement of mutual benefits to be gained and the costs to be incurred from this migration might open the way for a more effective policy based on regulating rather than restricting such migration. Such a system of regulated entry might imply some deregulation of the host labor market, allowing freer competition for those unskilled jobs that immigrants usually take up. But it should avoid the unfortunate and offensive discriminations of previous systems and instead strive to provide migrants with an acceptable work life and civil status in the host country. Such a system would, for instance, require legal equality, equality of economic treatment, and equality of opportunities for the migrant worker, as well as a series of some affirmative supports (opportunity to study the host country's language, for example, and training opportunities).

Regulating East–West Migration

The possibility of significant East–West migration has been created as a result of the transformation that is currently revolutionizing both the domestic economic and political arrangements within Eastern Europe and the relations of these states with the West. This migration also contains both real opportunities and real risks for (Western) labor.

Of course there has for some time been a continuing migration from East to West, but in years past this migration has been of a peculiar kind: virtually all of it has been under stimulus of political duress. Thus the migrants have been refugees, typically arriving with few possessions but highly committed to permanent relocation in the West. These migrants have often brought with them high levels of skills and training, and while constituting a relatively small absolute number, they have spread themselves thinly across many diverse final destinations (North America and Israel as well as Western Europe). Hence, the impact of these migrants on any particular set of national labor markets has been slight.

The reform process in the East opens up new possibilities for migration. The flow of migrants seeking employment in the West is likely to show a substantial increase simply as a function of the borders being more open, but there also exists the possibility that some of the Eastern European governments may encourage workers from the East to take up temporary employment in the West.[5] Some of the possibilities are as follows:

1. Most immediately, large-scale labor reallocations may occur within the newly unified German labor market, particularly if the transition process in the Eastern region results in an extended period of high unemployment. Moreover, the (formerly) East German labor force can now take advantage of its wider migration privileges within the European Community. Given the political and

economic unification of Germany, this migration will primarily be a matter for domestic German policy.

2. The prospect also exists for large labor migrations from Poland, Czechoslovakia, and Hungary. Whether such movements are realized depends, among other factors, on whether these governments can quickly generate significant economic growth, thereby providing substantial employment opportunities for their workers at home, and on the responsiveness of the West, and particularly the openness of the European Community, in permitting entry of migrating workers. Given the rather thoroughgoing political reforms evident in these countries, substantial labor migration from these countries is likely to be mostly economic in character, that is, migration made for the purpose of seeking improved employment opportunities but with the intention of being temporary in nature and with the migrants maintaining family and social ties and retaining political rights in their countries of origin.

3. Finally, the possibility also remains for greatly increased flows of workers from Romania, Bulgaria, Albania, and the Soviet Union. In these cases migration is likely to retain a strong political as well as economic stimulus. Like the conditions governing migrations from the other Eastern countries newly opened to market economies, whether the migrations from these countries become substantial in magnitude depends on whether these governments can stimulate rapid economic growth and employment at home and on how open the West will be to their migrants. But it also depends upon how thorough and complete the ongoing processes of political reform will be.

East–West migration represents something with a potential quite different from the South–North migrations.

First, it should be noted that despite the relatively back-
ward technology of industry in the East (in comparison
with its counterpart in the West), the labor force of the
East nonetheless is highly skilled. Levels of literacy, technical training, industrial experience, and advanced technical and scientific education and skills are all quite high.
Thus if a significant East–West migration were to develop,
it is highly likely that it would include substantial numbers
of skilled personnel. Already the European Community
has initiated steps to capitalize on this pool of skilled labor.
At their meeting in Strasbourg in December 1989, the
Council of Europe ministers announced their intention to
set up a European Vocational Training Foundation for
nationals from Eastern Europe.[6]

Second, some of the Eastern governments may be quite
attracted to permitting their workers to migrate to the
West on a temporary basis. There certainly would be
dangers and costs in such a policy for the governments of
the East: the economic difficulties of the East imply that
these countries will desperately need their skilled workers
at home; permitting migration to the West not only denies
the East this skilled labor while it is in the West, it
undoubtedly would risk losing it permanently. Moreover,
exposing workers to the higher living standards in the
West (and, for countries where the reform process fails to
be thoroughgoing, the freer political conditions in the
West) is likely to generate demands for more rapid im-
provements at home. On the other side, however, are the
attractions of such a policy: if there is substantial out-
migration, the size of the redundant labor pool at home is
reduced and at the same time the migrants can greatly
improve their living situations. And perhaps most appealing of all, allowing migration on a temporary basis may

prove to be a lucrative source of foreign exchange, through the mechanism of worker remittances.[7]

Thus the West, and particularly the European Community, confronts the possibility of a significant East–West migration. Given that an East–West migration is likely to be a movement of relatively highly skilled workers, and that employers in the West are likely to face increasing shortages (or more properly, a rising relative cost) of skilled labor, a Western opening to this migration would also seem highly appealing.

What, then, is labor's stake in this new East–West possibility? Surely labor's greatest stake, shared with the other social partners, is to assist the reform process in the East as part of strategy for enhancing world peace and security. In this endeavor, economic assistance, including some portion perhaps in the form of East-West migration and West-to-East remittances, makes sense. On the other side, those forms of economic assistance that serve directly to revive and stimulate growth within the Eastern economies themselves ought to have first priority, both because they are likely to be more efficient and because they will have the least adverse impact on Western labor.

More difficult are the issues of to what extent should migration be permitted, and to what extent will migration result in labor-market outcomes unfavorable to the interests of labor. It seems hard to deny that a substantial migration would have the effect of increasing competition for Western workers, including especially competition for the broad lower and middle ranges of occupations. Indeed, it is easy to envision a process whereby employers' sudden new access to the redundant labor supplies of the East (either in situ or as migrants) becomes the lever used to undermine labor conditions in the West. Thus the opening of the East could reinforce those problematical elements for labor in the realization of the Single Market, working to undercut both historical labor standards and the efficacy of the workers' organizations.

On the other hand, if the East–West flows are managed in such a way that sudden surpluses of skilled labor are avoided and that the migrants enter the world of labor on equal terms with existing workers (that is, they do not constitute a force undercutting the standards or working conditions of existing workers), then the infusion of talent from the East may well help fuel an economic boom that would benefit society at large, including both existing labor and migrants.

One key to the management of labor flows from the East is whether these flows are regulated as part of a long-run plan to integrate labor from the East or whether instead this regulation becomes part of domestic political bargaining and conflict within the West. Unless assured that the former will be true, the official labor organizations of the West are unlikely to be supportive of permitting heavy migrations. Again, the differences among the Western nations are great: Germany has a vast political and historical interest in making its reunification a success, and despite the huge economic impact from integration and migration, some of which is burdensome and negative, it approaches these questions with a different agenda than do the other Western nations. It will surely also have a different response to the integration of East labor pools from those of the other Western European countries.

Despite their differences, can the Western nations fashion a reasonably coherent strategy for developing relations with Middle and Eastern Europe that both sustains positive developments in the East and does not compromise

(Western) workers' interests? That must be the challenge put to policy-makers.

★   ★   ★

If the above considerations accurately sum up the dilemmas of South–North and East–West migrations, they suggest two further conclusions:

1. With respect to policies regulating migration in excess of the positive-sum-game level, (Northern or Western) labor has an interest in having migration policy understood as one among several development assistance alternatives; overreliance on this particular form of assistance may unduly penalize labor.

2. South–North and East–West migration is a policy area in which having multilateral agreement within the North concerning the regulation of such migration ought to be of the highest priority. The developed world in general has an obligation to assist the less developed world, yet the specific burden for each developed country of this general obligation is less clear. This raises the possibility of destructively competitive national policies. It is possible, for instance, for each separate country to interpret its own obligation in a niggardly way such that the total of the individual contributions sums to a level admitted by all to be too low. It is also possible for a country's employers or an interested subset of employers to use this opening aggressively to curtail the bargaining power of domestic workers by promoting an exaggerated level of migration.

In effect, the circumstance of a common obligation to be shared, with no mechanism to guarantee sharing, creates the need for a "social compact" among the developed countries to provide the discipline necessary to ensure that individual (national) obligations are met. Permitting migration from the South or the East in excess of the positive-sum-game level (and therefore implicitly as a development assistance measure) requires the same "social compact" model.

Establishing a multilateral approach to the recognition and regulation of clandestine migration is of particular significance. In the context of the European Single Market, such coordination is of course an essential precondition for any member state to be able to regulate such migration.[8] But even more generally, such coordination is the best avenue for removing migration policy from the arena of competitive, nationalistic, and domestic political considerations and instead placing it in a realm where labor's stake, as well as that of the other social partners and of the South and of the East, can be accommodated.

Notes

1. Japan, normally included in "the North" for most purposes, is here omitted only because it has rigorously excluded foreign labor; the presence of an apparently growing number of illegal foreign workers despite this policy suggests that only its exclusion policy prevents it from sharing the migrant situation of the other countries of the North.

2. Makis Cavouriaris, "Les Migrations Sud Nord" (*PerItaca Report*) p. 18. See also Michael Piore, *Birds of Passage: Migrant Labor and Industrial Societies* (Cambridge University Press: New York, 1979); George Borjas, *Friends or Strangers: The Impact of Immigrants on the U.S. Economy* (Basic Books: New York, 1990); Julian L. Simon, *The Economic Consequences of Immigration* (Basil Blackwell: Oxford, 1989).

3. See Dosi Giovanni, "Sources, Procedures, and Microeconomic Effects of Innovation," *Journal of Economic Literature*, vol. XXVI, no. 3 (September 1988), pp. 1120–171; Eileen Applebaum, "The Labor Market in Post-Keynesian Theory," in Michael Piore (ed.), *Unemployment and Inflation* (Sharpe: White Plains, N.Y., 1979), pp. 33–45.

4. G. Renshaw (ed.), *Employment, Trade and North-South Co-operation*

(ILO: Geneva, 1981); World Bank, *World Tables 1988–89* Edition (Johns Hopkins University Press: Baltimore, 1989).

5. New opportunities for a movement from West to East could also emerge, particularly for technical personnel, but it is unlikely that this migration would be significant in absolute terms.

6. Statement of the Council of Europe, Strasbourg, Dec. 10, 1989.

7. In this regard, see V. Grecic, "The Importance of Migrant Workers' and Emigrants' Remittances for the Yugoslav Economy," *International Migration—Migrations Internationales*, vol. XXVIII, no. 2 (June 1990) pp. 201–13.

8. The EC Commission has proposed various guidelines in this regard.

6

Summary and Conclusions

WORKERS IN THE DEVELOPED countries are facing a new set of world economic relationships, and these relationships are increasingly shaped by the processes of international economic integration. The interests of the world of labor, as the interests of other constituencies in these societies, are being profoundly reshaped and transformed by these processes.

Labor's interests are, at bottom, simple, abiding, and unchanged: workers seek to improve the fundamental terms and conditions under which they labor for their livings. They seek security of employment, adequate recompense for their labors, dignity in their work lives, protection from occupational hazards and accidents, diverse and fulfilling work, sustenance during unemployment or ill health, opportunities for personal growth, support in old age, and identity and integration into the surrounding community. These interests have not changed.

What has changed and is changing is the economic world in which labor works and lives—the circumstances in which workers seek to meet their needs and realize their dreams. What has for some generations been an aggregation of national economies, albeit with important regional autonomies and international aspects, is rapidly becoming integrated into a distinct pattern of transnational market blocs. We do not argue that the world is becoming one marketplace; rather, that the effective economic units—the European Single Market, North America, the trans-Pacific trading partners—are increasingly transnational and that these major blocs are themselves becoming increasingly knitted together in reciprocal economic relationships. In short, the economic world in which workers must seek to advance and defend their interests can no longer be appropriately conceived of in national units.

Workers' efforts to control the terms and conditions under which they labor are, as always, relative. As but one of the elements of social production, and as but one of the constituencies of civil society, labor necessarily coexists with, cooperates with, and works alongside the other elements in the productive process and the other social partners in society. While its interests are in some ways distinct from the interests of the other social partners, in crucial ways labor also shares with them in the benefits and burdens experienced by society at large.

In the past, labor has sought to defend and advance its interests through two primary mechanisms: national labor unions and social democratic state politics. In varying combinations, with varying degrees of cooperation or confrontation, and with varying levels of success, national confederations of unions and national democratic parties in the advanced countries have led the struggles for better working conditions, more adequate pay, safer workplaces, greater social security, and the other economic and social benefits that labor has achieved.

These traditional forms of advancing workers' interests will remain important, even primary, in the years ahead. Yet inevitably their effectiveness declines as the transnational character of the economic world becomes more prominent. Thus we must also consider what is labor's stake in our increasingly integrated transnational economy, and how labor's interests will be defended and advanced. Hence the concerns raised in this book, which have, ultimately, to do with issues of freedom and control.

One issue of freedom and control concerns where a person may work and what constraints will be imposed on a worker who chooses to move across a national boundary. Geographic mobility is one of the most fundamental freedoms of free labor, and today's efforts to dismantle the barriers to mobility are not dissimilar from the serfs' struggles a few centuries ago to be free to choose where to work.

Labor's freedom to move has traditionally been held hostage to larger political strategies. During the first half of this century, the advanced world was divided among highly rivalrous nation-state economies, and so labor's freedom to move was restricted for nationalist reasons. During the second half of this century, the advanced world was divided between warring capitalist and socialist camps, and so labor's freedom to move was restricted for ideological reasons. As we now move toward political arrangements that are less directly aggrandizing and an economy that is far more internationally integrated, perhaps it is time to remove the geographical shackles from labor.

A second issue of freedom and control is labor's ability to ensure local economic relationships that sustain and foster workers' sense of identity, of place, of community, uniqueness, and belongingness. To what extent will workers control or influence those forces impinging upon individual workplaces? Will they wield or be deprived of the tools needed to maintain (or alter) those circumstances that make individual workplaces unique, special, and satisfying? The concerns here have to do with technology and its manifest applications, and whether these applications will work to sustain workers in their efforts to maintain the integratedness of their work and their lives. These concerns also have to do with the role of locale and region in the larger agendas of corporations, national governments, and international agencies, and whether from their Olympian heights these centralized institutions can and will sustain workers in their need to extract meaning and purpose from their work lives. As the economy develops toward a more integrated international system, perhaps special attention should be paid to preserving and extending those local and cultural features of work relationships that give people identity, fulfillment, and pride.

A third issue has to do with managing the current and potential large migrations from South to North and East to West. Even as the countries of North America, Japan, and Western Europe struggle to devise a system for managing the growing integration of economic relations among themselves, and even if they were to incorporate into their policies those elements needed to accommodate indigenous labor's legitimate interests within the processes of integration, the pressure of urgent and unmet needs and dramatically changing circumstances in the South and the East confronts and will increasingly confront the advanced countries with a great demand for in-migration. How will this demand be met, and whose interests will be served by the answers? Labor in the advanced countries also has a great stake in these questions, although as we have tried to argue (but labor's offical representatives sometimes tend to forget), labor's interest need not be understood as either selfishly narrow-minded nor as reactionary. As pressures for migration (both legal and clandestine) from the East and the South become more intense, perhaps policy-makers in the advanced countries should seize the opportunity to expand the area of win–win solutions by devising and implementing a multilateral and comprehensive strategy of cooperation with the South and the East.

The three issues discussed above, although they have absorbed our attention herein, do not represent the full range of labor's interests in the processes and consequences of international economic integration. Indeed, two others, not considered here, have traditionally been the center of focus: labor's direct interest in the employment consequences of coordinated macroeconomic policy; and the question of how national systems of collective bargaining will operate within a labor market that is increasingly international. And still other issues beckon: the occupational health and safety consequences of new technologies that are increasingly transnational; the employment consequences of trade policies and of transnational employers' strategies; the consequences for family life, child care, and personal support of employer personnel systems that are increasingly internationally based; and on and on, through the full range of concerns and consequences that appropriately emerge when labor, both a factor of production and a fundamental part of our lives, is understood in its proper perspective. All of these issues come into view when we pose for serious consideration these questions: How can workers gain from increased economic integration? What truly is labor's stake in international economic cooperation?

With respect to each of these issues, as we have noted, labor's effort must be to achieve a degree of influence and participation sufficient to defend and advance its stake in these matters. Labor struggled through much of the nineteenth and twentieth centuries to achieve its status as an accepted social partner, a real player in the governance of national economies and national destinies. The primary lesson to be taken from labor's struggles in this regard is that its success, while undoubtedly highly beneficial to its own interests, turned out not to be damaging to the interests of the other social partners. Indeed, quite the opposite: the last forty-five years, the years of labor's greatest participation in the governance of the developed nations, has also been a period of peace among the major powers and sustained prosperity for all of the major industrial economies and for all of the social partners.

In the new context of a transnational economy, labor must again find its legitimate place and voice among the social partners. This will not be easy. Despite some openings and efforts at international cooperation, unions and social democratic parties have remained largely national creatures, organized along national lines and responding to national pressures. Thus the precise form of labor's entrance into the company of international social partners remains uncertain, and what organization can give voice to labor's interests remains to be determined.[1]

But the lesson from the national experiences seems relevant. Labor's stake propels it to take its rightful place in the determination of international policy. And if it does, why should we expect that its admission will do otherwise than repeat at the international level the beneficial effects that its entrance on the national stages produced for national economies? The forgotten link must be remembered, and the sooner labor's stake in international economic cooperation is recognized, the sooner our emerging economic world may be shaped to better ends.

Note

1. Among other items, see Confédération Européenne des Syndicats, "Creating the European Social Dimension in the Internal Market," Executive Committee statement, adopted on Dec. 11–12, 1988; Trades Union Congress, *Maximising the Benefits, Minimising the Costs: TUC Report on Europe, 1992* (Trades Union Congress: London, 1988); Wolfgang Hager, "1992: What About the Workers?" *The International Economy*, vol. III, no. 2 (March-April 1989), pp. 84–88; Confédération Générale du Travail, "La CGT et L'Europe," CGT Secteur International, October 1988; Denis MacShane, "Trade Unions in Europe in the 1990's: Challenges, Opportunities and Dangers" (International Metalworkers Federation: Geneva, Mar. 17, 1989).

Bibliography

Abowd, John, and Richard Freeman, "The Internationalization of the U.S. Labor Market," NBER Working Paper No. 3321 (National Bureau of Economic Research: Cambridge, Mass., April 1990).

Applebaum, Eileen, "The Labor Market in Post-Keynesian Theory," in Michael Piore (ed.), *Unemployment and Inflation* (Sharpe: White Plains, N.Y., 1979).

Barnouin, Barbara, *The European Labour Movement and European Integration* (Pinter: London, 1986).

Belous, Richard, and Rebecca Hartley (eds.), *The Growth of Regional Trading Blocs in the Global Economy* (NPA Publications: Washington, D.C., 1990).

Bluestone, Barry, and Bennett Harrison, *The Deindustrialization of America* (Basic Books: New York, 1984).

Borjas, George, *Friends or Strangers: The Impact of Immigrants on the U.S. Economy* (Basic Books: New York, 1990).

Borzaga, Carlo, and Raffaele Brancati, "L'impatto della Cooperazione Economica Internazionale sulle Economie Locali," in Paolo Garonna and Richard Edwards, (eds.), *PerItaca Report*, 1990.

Brubaker, William Rogers, "Immigration and the Politics of Citizenship," *TransAtlantic Perspectives*, no. 20 (Autumn 1989).

—— (ed.), *Immigration and the Politics of Citizenship in Europe and North America* (University Press of America: New York, 1989).

———, "Membership without Citizenship: The Economic and Social Rights of Noncitizens," in William Rogers Brubaker (ed.), *Immigration and the Politics of Citizenship in Europe and North America*, 1989.

Brusco, S., "Labour Market Structure, Company Policies and Technological Progress: The Case of Italy," in O. Diettrich and J. Morley, (eds.), *Relations between Technology Capital and Labour* (Commission of the European Communities: Brussels, 1981).

Brusco, S., and C. Sabel, "Artisan Production and Economic Growth," in F. Wilkinson (ed.), *The Dynamics of Labour Market Segmentation* (Academic Press: London, 1981).

Butcher, Paul, and Joseph Erdos, "International Social Security Agreements: The U.S. Experience," *Social Security Bulletin*, vol. 51, no. 9 (September 1988).

Butera, F., "Mutamento dell'organizzazione del lavoro ed egemonia," *Economia e Lavoro*, vol. VIII, no. 1, January–February 1974.

Cavouriaris, Makis, "Les Migrations Sud Nord," in Paolo Garonna and Richard Edwards, (eds.), *PerItaca Report*, 1990.

Commission of the European Communities, *Communications from the EEC Concerning the Action Programme Relating to the Implementation of the Community Charter of Basic Social Rights for Workers* (EEC: Brussels, November 1989).

——— (Commissione della CEE), *Efficienza Stabilità ed Equità, Una Strategia per l'evoluzione del sistema economico della Comunità Europea*, Padoa Schioppa Report (EEC, Il Mulino: Bologna, 1988).

———, *The European Challenge 1992, The Benefits of a Single Market*, Report of the Research Group on the "Costs of Non-Europe," Cecchini Report, 1988 (French edition by Flammarion: Paris; Italian edition by Sperling and Kupfer: Milano).

———, *Social Dimension of the Internal Market*, Marin Report, EEC (88) 1148 (mimeo), (EEC: Brussels, Sept. 14, 1988).

Communiqués of the G-7 economic summit meetings, 1982 to 1990.

Confédération Européenne des Syndicats, "Creating the European Social Dimension in the Internal Market," Executive Committee statement, Brussels, Feb. 11–12, 1988.

Confédération Générale du Travail, "La CGT et L'Europe," CGT Secteur International, Paris, October 1988.

Council of Europe, "Statement", Strasbourg, Dec. 10, 1989.

———, *Explanatory Reports on the European Convention on Social Security and on the Supplementary Agreement for the Application of the European Convention on Social Security* (Council of Europe: Strasbourg, 1973).

Council of Ministers, European Community, "Statement", Hannover, June 1988.

Creutz, Helmut, "The I.L.O. and Social Security for Foreign and Migrant Workers," *International Labour Review*, vol. 97, no. 4 (April 1968).

Di Nunzio, Potito, "Il Trattamento Fiscale per i Lavoratori all'Estero," *Diritto & Pratica del Lavoro*, no. 10 (1985).

Duda, Helga, and Franz Tödtling, "Austrian Trade Unions in the Economic Crisis," in R. Edwards, P. Garonna, and F. Tödtling (eds.), *Unions in Crisis and Beyond: Perspectives from Six Countries*, 1986.

Edwards, Richard, *Rights at Work: New Public Policy Strategies towards Workplace Rights* (forthcoming).

Edwards, Richard, and S. Bowles, *Understanding Capitalism* (Harper and Row: New York, 1985), Chapter 9.

Edwards, R., P. Garonna, and F. Tödtling (eds.), *Unions in Crisis and Beyond: Perspectives from Six Countries* (Auburn House: Dover, Mass., 1986).

European Economic Community, *Social Europe*, Special Number, Office of Official Publications (EEC: Luxembourg, 1988).

Gaja, di Giorgio, *I Lavoratori Stranieri in Italia* (Il Mulino: Bologna, 1984).

Garonna, Paolo, and Richard Edwards, *The Forgotten Link: Labor's Stake in International Economic Cooperation* (PerItaca Report), (PerItaca: Rome, 1990).

Gill, Ken, "Europe 1992: The British Response," *Economic Notes* (Labor Research Association), vol. 58, no. 5–6 (May-June 1990).

Giovanni, Dosi, "Sources, Procedures, and Microeconomic Effects of Innovation," *Journal of Economic Literature*, vol. XXVI, no. 3 (September 1988).

Gordon, David, "The Global Economy: New Edifice or Crumbling Foundations?" *New Left Review*, no. 168 (March-April 1988).

Grasselli, Sergio, "Il Lavoro Italiano all'Estero," *Diritto & Pratica del Lavoro*, no. 41 (1986).

Grecic, V., "The Importance of Migrant Workers' and Emigrants' Remittances for the Yugoslav Economy," *International Migration—Migrations Internationales*, vol. XXVIII, no. 2 (June 1990).

Hager, Wolfgang, "1992: What about the Workers?" *The International Economy*, vol. III, no. 2 (March-April 1989).

Hufbauer, Gary Clyde, *Europe 1992: An American Perspective* (Brookings: Washington, D.C., 1990).

International Labor Conference, *Convention 118* (Convention Concerning Equality of Treatment of Nationals and Non-Nationals in Social Security), 46th Session of the International Labor Organization (ILO: Geneva, June 1962).

————, *Convention 157* (Convention Concerning the Establishment of an International System for the Maintenance of Rights in Social Security), 68th Session of the International Labor Organization (ILO: Geneva, June 1982).

————, *Maintenance of Migrant Workers' Rights in Social Security* (Revision of Convention 48), 67th Session, Report VII(i) (ILO: Geneva, 1981).

————, *Social Security Protection in Old-Age*, General Survey of the Committee of Experts on the Application of Conventions and Recommendations, International Labor Conference, 76th Session (ILO: Geneva, 1989).

International Labor Organization, *Into the Twenty-First Century: The Development of Social Security* (ILO: Geneva, 1984).

————, *Liste des instruments internationaux de sécurité sociale* (ILO: Geneva, 1984).

————, *Social Security for Migrant Workers* (ILO: Geneva, 1977).

International Monetary Fund, *World Economic Outlook* (IMF: Washington D.C., 1986).

Kenan, Peter, *The International Economy*, 2nd ed. (Prentice-Hall: Englewood Cliffs, N.J., 1989).

Koechlin, Timothy, "Labor, Technological Change, and International Economic Integration," in Paolo Garonna and Richard Edwards, (eds.), *PerItaca Report*, 1990.

Lawrence, Robert Z., and Robert Litan, *Saving Free Trade: A Pragmatic Approach* (Brookings: Washington, D.C., 1986).

MacShane, Denis, "Trade Unions in Europe in the 1990's—Challenges, Opportunities and Dangers" (mimeo; International Metalworkers Federation: Geneva, March 1989).

Marsden, David, and Paul Ryan, "The Transferability of Skills and the Mobility of Skilled Workers in the European Community," in Paolo Garonna and Richard Edwards, (eds.), *PerItaca Report*, 1990.

Marshall, Ray, *Unheard Voices: Labor and Economic Policy in a Competitive World* (Basic Books: New York, 1987).

Mishel, Lawrence, "The Late Great Debate on Deindustrialization," *Challenge*, vol. 32, no. 1 (January–February 1989).

Molle, Willem, and Aad van Mourik, "International Movements of Labour under Conditions of Economic Integration: The Case of Western Europe," *Journal of Common Market Studies*, vol. XXVI, no. 3 (March 1988).

Organization for Economic Cooperation and Development, *The Future of Social Protection*, Social Security Studies, no. 6 (OECD: Paris, 1988).

———, *Labour Force Statistics 1967–1987* (OECD: Paris, 1989).

———, *Labour Market Flexibility: The Current Debate*, Dahrendorf Report, Report of a High Group of Experts (OECD: Paris, 1986).

———, *New Technologies in the 1990's, A Socio-Economic Strategy*, Sundqvist Report, Report of a High Group of Experts (OECD: Paris, 1988).

———, *Reforming Public Pensions*, Social Policy Studies, no. 5 (OECD: Paris, 1988).

———, *SOPEMI 1987* (OECD: Paris, 1988).

———, *SOPEMI 1988* (OECD: Paris, 1989).

Piore, Michael, *Birds of Passage: Migrant Labor and Industrial Societies* (Cambridge University Press: New York, 1979).

Piore, Michael, and Charles Sabel, *The Second Industrial Divide* (Basic Books: New York, 1984).

Plant, R., *Industries in Trouble* (ILO: Geneva, 1981).

Renshaw, G. (ed.), *Employment, Trade and North–South Co-operation* (ILO: Geneva, 1981).

Schuck, Peter, "Membership in the Liberal Polity: The Devaluation of American Citizenship," in William Rogers Brubaker (ed.), *Immigration and the Politics of Citizenship in Europe and North America*, 1989.

Simon, Julian L., *The Economic Consequences of Immigration* (Basil Blackwell: Oxford, 1989).

Standing, Guy, *Unemployment and Labour Market Flexibility: SWEDEN* (ILO: Geneva, 1988).

Straubhaar, Thomas, "International Labour Migration within a Common Market: Some Aspects of EC Experience," *Journal of Common Market Studies*, vol. XXVII, no. 1 (September 1988).

Teague, Paul, and John Grahl, "European Community Labour Market Policy: Present Scope and Future Direction," *Revue d'Intégration européenne*, vol. XIII, no. 1 (Automne 1989).

Trades Union Congress, *Maximising the Benefits, Minimising the Costs: TUC Report on Europe 1992* (Trades Union Congress: London, August 1988).

United Nations, *Trade and Development Report, 1987* (UN: New York, 1987).

U.S. Bureau of the Census, *Migration between the United States and Canada*, Current Population Reports, Series P-23 (U.S. GPO: Washington, D.C., 1990).

U.S. President, *Economic Report of the President, 1989* (U.S. GPO: Washington, D.C., January 1989).

Villars, C., "Social Security for Migrant Workers in the Framework of the Council of Europe," *International Labour Review*, vol. 120, no. 3 (May-June 1981).

World Bank, *World Development Report 1988* (World Bank: Washington, D.C., 1988).

———, *World Tables 1988–89 Edition* (Johns Hopkins University Press: Baltimore, 1989).

Index

About the Authors

RICHARD EDWARDS is professor and chairman in the Department of Economics at the University of Massachusetts, Amherst. He received his Ph.D. from Harvard University in 1972, and is the prize-winning author or co-author of nine books and over thirty scholarly articles, including *Contested Terrain: The Transformation of the Workplace in the Twentieth Century* and *Unions in Crisis and Beyond: Perspectives from Six Countries*. He was a member in Social Science at the Institute for Advanced Study (Princeton) and has served as a panel member for the National Academy of Sciences and research economist for the National Bureau of Economic Research. He is the president of the Institute for Economic Studies (Amherst). His current work focuses on changes in workplace relations during the current international process of industrial restructuring. He lives in Amherst with his wife and three children.

PAOLO GARONNA is deputy director of Manpower, Social Affairs, and Education at the Organization for Economic

Cooperation and Development in Paris. He also holds the Chair of Applied Economics at the Faculty of Statistics at the University of Padua. A native of Rome, he studied at the University of Rome, University of Denver, and Cambridge University. He is the author or co-author of some eighty research papers and publications, including *Cassa Integrazione Guadagni,* which was awarded the Tarantelli Prize. He has served as economic adviser to the Italian Labor Minister, Finance Minister, and Treasury Minister, and he was a member of the Comitato Technico per la Politica Economica e Sociale. He is the president of Per-Itaca, s.r.l. He lives in Paris with his wife and three children.